THEY LED A NATION

by
Virginia Driving Hawk Sneve

Portraits by
Loren Zephier

Brevet Press, Inc.
Sioux Falls, South Dakota

Published by Brevet Press, Inc.
Copyright © 1975 by BREVET PRESS, INC.
Sioux Falls, South Dakota 57101

Library of Congress Catalog Card Number: 75-254

Hard Cover Edition
ISBN: 88498-026-X

Soft Cover Edition
ISBN: 88498-027-8

All rights reserved.
No part of this work nor its format covered by the copyright hereon may be reproduced or used in any form or by any means—graphic, electronic or mechanical, including photocopying, recording, taping or information storage retrieval systems—without written permission of the publisher.

First Printing 1975
Second Printing 1982
Third Printing 1987
Manufactured in the United States of America
Printed by Pine Hill Press
Freeman, South Dakota

They Led A Nation

Introduction

Each nation on earth has found the need to be directed within the ideals of its culture inescapable. In times of crisis leaders emerge from the general population to protect that which makes this culture unique in the eyes of history. So is it true of the Sioux Indians.

The Sioux leaders were men—men who knew joy, heartbreak, fear, and courage. As with leaders of all races, some were benevolent patriarchs and others despotic sadists. These men and their actions guided American history on a course which would have been vastly different if the Sioux leaders had not lived. Yet they did live. Some were thrust into history by events beyond their control. Others sought their role for a strong purpose, or even in the name of divine guidance. These men, weak and strong, led the Sioux Nation.

The word "chief" is retained in this book because it is the label used and understood by non-Indians when speaking of Indian leaders. The term is not Indian. The word "chief" has become so identified with the native American that its mere utterance provokes a picture of stoic greatness, unflinching courage and perfect examples of manly beauty and strength. To use another word for these men would be to rob them of their glory and confuse the reader.

Some of the leaders in this book were hereditary chiefs—the role passed from father to son in dynasties as regal as European royalty. The difference was that if a Sioux chief was not an effective leader, another emerged and assumed the power with the consent of the people without bloody civil strife. Nor did a chief have supreme authority. Decisions affecting the whole band or tribe were made with the advice of a council of wiser, more experienced elders.

SIOUX is also retained as the generic name for the best known Indian inhabitants of South Dakota. Among the SIOUX people there is pride in wanting to be called by their true name, but the author may not call all of the chiefs LAKOTA, for they are not. Neither may they all be called DAKOTA for the same reason.

The chiefs selected for the biographic and portrait sketches in this book were not chosen with any great design. All had a strong sense of the dramatic, were intelligent, imaginative men who knew and fully understood the mystic element of the Sioux culture. There were many other leaders who rose and fell in history's overwhelming tide and their absence from this work does not negate their importance or greatness as leaders.

The Sioux history was an oral one and often is in conflict with the written records of white historians. Time had a different meaning to the Indian and was of lesser importance to the incidents that dramatically affected their lives. When such were reported to white historians, who then had to interpret and set dates, conflicting information was recorded. Therefore, few of the men in this book have accurately recorded birthdates, and even their deaths, most of which occurred after white men became a permanent part of their land, are often speculated.

This conflict of data extends to the recorded likenesses from which the portraits in this book were drawn. Sitting Bull, for example, is a face well known to Americans. However, pictures of other chiefs have been identified as the likeness of more than one man.

Included in this book is the biographical essay of Crazy Horse, but there is no portrait sketch. Legend has it that there was no sketch or photograph ever made of this Sioux leader, although there have been contrary claims in recent years. The Sioux people, themselves, to this day wish this great hero to remain in "faceless anonymity" to forever symbolize the "disgrace and dishonor of their defeat and the need for inspired leaders to direct them again to the glory they once knew."

The author,
Virginia Driving Hawk Sneve

Contents

"for we have been forever in the land..."
   (a brief history) 1

The Red Wing Dynasty 4

Shakopee I, II, III 6

Tamaha 8

Struck By The Ree 10

Little Crow 12

Little Thunder 14

Inkpaduta 16

Martin Charger 18

Gall 20

Man Afraid of His Horses 22

Red Cloud 24

Crazy Horse 26

Sitting Bull 28

Hump 30

Short Bull 32

Gabriel Renville 34

Spotted Tail 36

American Horse 38

Blue Cloud 40

Big Foot 42

Bibliography 44

Index 45

Seven Council Fires

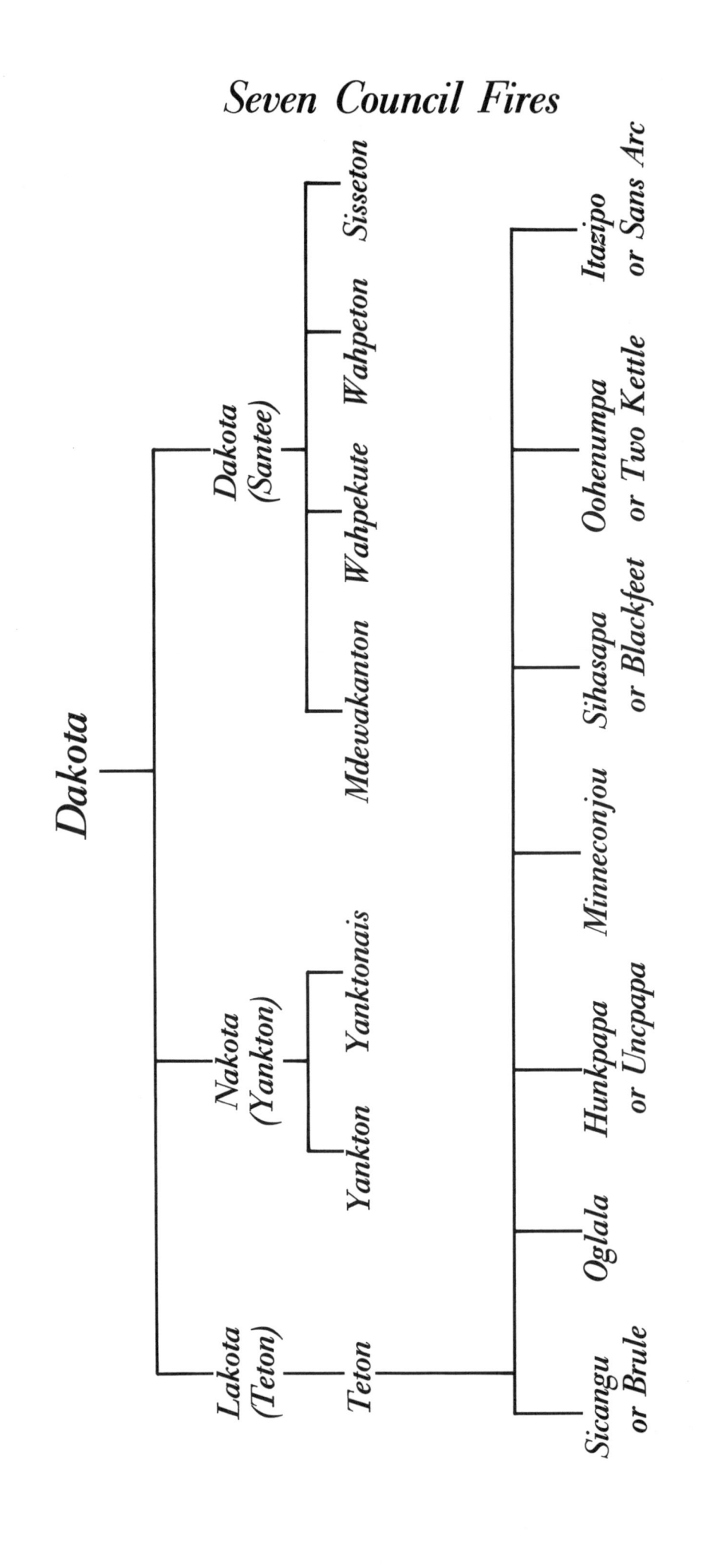

Dakota
- Lakota (Teton)
  - Teton
    - Sicangu or Brule
    - Oglala
    - Hunkpapa or Uncpapa
    - Minneconjou
    - Sihasapa or Blackfeet
    - Oohenumpa or Two Kettle
    - Itazipo or Sans Arc
- Nakota (Yankton)
  - Yankton
  - Yanktonais
- Dakota (Santee)
  - Mdewakanton
  - Wahpekute
  - Wahpeton
  - Sisseton

"for we have been forever in the land and forever will remain"

Sioux tradition places their nation's beginning north of the mouth of the Mississippi River around the Mille Lacs of northern Minnesota. Where their ancestors lived before that is not known to the Sioux, nor does it matter to them, "for we have been forever in the land and forever will remain."

Ethnological theories written by white scholars assume the Sioux to be placed within the Mongolian emigrations from the north and west, or within later emigrations from South America.

The first mention of the Sioux Nation in recorded history was in 1640 by Jean Nicolet. Nicolet noted the Sioux as living near the Winnebagos. In 1641, Jesuit missionaries heard from the Chippewas of the Nadewisou tribe who lived eighteen days to the west and beyond the great lakes. Pierre Radisson mentions the Nadewisou in his visits in 1654-59. Other tribes of the region, Objibwa (Chippewa) and Huron, expressed great fear of the Nadewisou to the French fur trader Radisson. With the first few sentences jotted down in a French fur trader—explorer's diary the best known Indian inhabitants of the United States Upper Midwest have suffered an unwanted nickname.

The French called these people SIOUX which is a derivative of the Chippewa word, NADEWISOU. The Chippewa were their sworn enemies. NADEWISOU means "treacherous snake". Naturally the Sioux prefer their own ancient traditional name of DAKOTA. DAKOTA means "friends" or an "alliance of friends". This traditional name is derived from the Santee, DAKOTA, koda, or from the Teton, LAKOTA, kola.

The French were the first to frequently contact the Sioux, often being trapped in the midst of the bloody conflict between the Sioux and their traditional enemies, the Chippewa. The Chippewa successfully pushed the Sioux from the lake lands because they were the first to learn how to use firearms effectively. The guns were traded from the French for furs.

The first white men found the Dakota in large numbers still living in the lake lands, using wild rice as a vital part of their food supply. These were the Santee. The Teton, Yankton and Yanktonais had already left and moved onto the plains. At this time (1700s) the Dakota were divided into seven closely related tribes and joined in an alliance of the Seven Council Fires for their mutual protection. The tribes were MDEWAKANTON (M'deh-wah-kahn-ton), WAHPEKUTE (Wah-peh-coo-tey), WAHPETON (Wah-peh-ton), SISSETON (Sis-sey-ton), YANKTON (Yank-ton), YANKTONAIS (Yank-toh-nays), and TETON (Tee-tahn). They named themselves, or each other, for the region they inhabited or after a peculiar characteristic. All but one of the names have the TON ending which came from OTONWAHE (Oh-toon-wah-hey), which meant "village or place where the people dwell."

The first four were collectively called ISANTI, "knife", because these people once lived near a large body of water, MDEISANTI, Knife Lake. The French later changed ISANTI to SANTEE. The Santee, who were the last to leave the lake region, speak the Dakota dialect in which there are no l's and the d is used.

The Yankton were originally one tribe but economic reasons forced their division into two groups as they became more populous. Their name, "dwellers on the end", referred to their custom of always camping at the end of the horn-shaped camp circle during great Dakota encampments. The YANKTONAIS name translates as "little Yankton". These people were sometimes called WICIYELA (Wik-che-yea-lah) or "middle people" because they lived between the Santee and the Tetons. They speak the NAKOTA dialect which uses the n in the place of the d.

The TETON, "dwellers on the plains", were the first to move to the prairie. After the move was made, the Teton became so numerous that they in turn divided into seven sub-tribes: SICANGU or Brule, SIHASAPA or Blackfeet, OOHENUMPA or Two Kettle, OGLALA, HUNKPAPA or UNCPAPA, MINNECONJOU and ITAZIPO or SANS ARC. The Teton dialect is LAKOTA, which uses the l in place of the d.

When the Teton Sioux began their westward movement they found the Iowas and Omahas in the lands adjacent to the Mississippi River, so they moved southwest and first lived around Big Stone Lake. The Yanktons followed but they went south and at the beginning of the 18th Century were at home in what is now the western part of Iowa. The Chippewas continued to press the Sioux out of the Minnesota woodlands and the Sioux in turn drove the Iowas away from the Minnesota Valley and the Omahas from the Sioux River and James River Valleys. The Teton claimed these lands as their hunting grounds.

The far-ranging Teton found that the lands west of the Missouri River did not have the heavy snowfall as on the eastern side. This meant that the buffalo herds wintered in plenty on the Western Plains. About 1760 the Sioux moved from Big Stone Lake, the Sioux River and the James River Valleys to the Missouri River. The Missouri River Valley was inhabited then by the Arikara (Ree) Indians who were an agrarian tribe. The Teton, at this time, became masters of the horse and a new nomadic culture of dreams and song began. By 1792, the Arikara were forced to abandon their homes in what is now South Dakota state and move north of the Grand River to North Dakota.

The Yanktons followed the Teton who supplied them with horses and they moved into the James River Valley. The Sisseton Santee came to the former Teton home at Big Stone Lake.

All of South Dakota, half of Minnesota, much of North Dakota, parts of Wisconsin and Iowa was the Sioux Nation. However, the Teton roamed further and were known to have visited the Gulf of Mexico, Hudson's Bay, the Alleghenies and the Rocky Mountains.

A chronology of the events noted throughout the biographical sketches follows:

Pontiac War, 1763—An Indian alliance under the Ottawa leader, Pontiac, held off the British for three years from the Illinois country and the Great Lakes.

American Revolutionary War, 1776—In this war most of the Sioux (Santee) involved were British allies.

Pike's Treaty of 1805—This was the first treaty between the United States of America and the Sioux Indians in which the Santee ceded land at the mouth of the St. Croix River and at the junction of the Minnesota and Mississippi for the establishment of military forts in exchange for $2,000.00.

Prairie du Chien Council, 1825—At this great gathering of many tribes, an arbitrary boundary line was set up by the United States to end hostilities between the Sioux and Chippewa.

Treaty of Traverse des Sioux, 1851—At this treaty the Santeee gave up lands in Minnesota, Iowa and Dakota and agreed to move to a reservation along the Minnesota River.

Treaty of Mendota, 1851—Essentially the same as the Traverse des Sioux Treaty.

Treaty of Fort Laramie, 1851—The United States thought the Teton and other plains tribes had pledged eternal peace among themselves.

Ash Hollow Massacre, 1855—At this site General Harney's troops treacherously ambushed a Brule band.

Yankton Treaty, 1858—The Yankton ceded all lands between the Big Sioux and Missouri Rivers and moved to a 400,000 acre reservation.

Minnesota Uprising, 1862—Santee tribes, unhappy after years of broken promises, delayed annuities, and strife among themselves brought on by the whites, rose against the settlers and soldiers in the Minnesota Valley.

Sisseton Treaty, 1867—The Sisseton Wahpeton Santee agreed to the boundaries of their reservation.

Red Cloud's War, 1866-68—Red Cloud opposed the opening of the Bozeman Trail to travel by whites and the staffing of forts in the traditional hunting lands of the Teton. For two years he led the Oglalas and other Teton bands in battles against the United States Army and forced the abandonment of the forts.

Laramie Treaty, 1868—This treaty confirmed a permanent reservation for the Sioux in all of South Dakota west of the Missouri River and the Indians in turn released all lands east of the Missouri except the Crow Creek, Sisseton and Yankton Reservations. In this treaty the government promised that no whites would enter the Sioux reservation without the Sioux's permission and that further negotiations must be ratified by the signatures of three-fourths of the adult Sioux males.

Black Hills War, 1876—In 1871 - 73 surveyors for the Northern Pacific Railroad invaded the Sioux Reservation without permission. In 1874, Custer led an illegal expedition into the Black Hills and discovered gold. This led to a stampede of illegal entries into Sioux land by gold seekers. All were in violation of the 1868 Treaty. The Sioux were determined to enforce the terms even if the United States would not. Notable Sioux victories were at the Battle of the Rosebud on June 17, 1876, and at the Little Big Horn on June 25, 1876. General Crook pursued the Sioux after the Little Big Horn and finally caught a band at Slim Buttes on September 17, 1876.

Treaty of 1889—This treaty was negotiated at the different agencies on the Sioux Reservation. Coercion, threats and force were used to obtain Sioux signatures and was in open violation of the 1868 Treaty for three-fourths of the adult Sioux males did not sign. By terms of this treaty all lands between the White and Cheyenne Rivers—(South Dakota) all of what was to become Perkins and Harding Counties, portions of Meade and Butte Counties north of the Belle Fourche River was open to the whites.

Massacre at Wounded Knee, December 29, 1890—The tragic culmination of white men's fear that the Sioux's desperate belief in the Ghost Dance Religion would lead to an uprising.

THE RED WING DYNASTY
Mdewakanton Santee

The Santee chiefs who bore the name of Red Wing were named so after a family talisman—a swan wing dyed red. The talisman was passed on from father to son for generations. The Red Wing Band made their home on the west shore of Lake Pepin, Minnesota. The present Red Wing, Minnesota, on that same shore, was named in honor of these chiefs.

The first RED WING was known in recorded history as early as the Pontiac War, 1763, when he visited Mackinaw, Michigan. Later, Red Wing allied himself with the British Red Coats and fought against the independence-seeking colonists of the American Revolution. Red Wing's son, TATANKAMANI, Walking Buffalo, followed, and he too, was a British ally during the War of 1812.

On his journey north to discover the headwaters of the Mississippi River, Lieutenant Zebulon Montgomery Pike met Walking Buffalo in 1805 at the Lake Pepin village. Pike spoke and wrote well of Walking Buffalo saying that he was a handsome, intelligent man who had the respect of all the Santee.

Walking Buffalo signed the Treaty at the Portages des Sioux in 1815. He also attended the Chippewa-Sioux Boundary Conference in 1825 at Prairie du Chien, Wisconsin. This conference ended through adjustment of tribal boundaries the hereditary war between the Sioux and Chippewa, confirming Sioux possession of an immense territory. This area included nearly half of Minnesota, two-thirds of the Dakotas and large portions of Wisconsin, Iowa, Missouri and Wyoming.

Shortly after refusing to sign the Treaty of 1837 in which the strip of land on both sides of the Mississippi River between the Iowa state line and St. Paul, Minnesota, would be ceded to the whites, Walking Buffalo died. Legend has it that he was buried astride his horse on a bluff overlooking the Red Wing Village.

Walking Buffalo was the father of Winona Crawford who married a scotch trader. Their daughter was the mother of Gabriel Renville (page 34).

WACOUTA, the Shooter, succeeded Walking Buffalo and was also one of the signers of the Traverse des Sioux Treaty in 1851. In that year the greater part of Minnesota was sold, but the dissatisfaction in the government's delay in fulfilling their terms of the sale led to hostilities between the Indians and the white soldiers and settlers. The hostilities began in 1857, six years after the treaty was signed. During this time, Wacouta moved his band to the reservation and settled near Chief Wabasha east of the agency.

Although he opposed the Minnesota Uprising of the Santee in 1862, Wacouta led his band in battles against the whites. Wacouta feared losing his power over the Santee and being considered a traitor more than he opposed the slaughter of nearly 800 white settlers in the bloody uprising also referred to as the Minnesota Massacre.

Moving with many other Santee to a northern Nebraska reservation after the Uprising of 1862, Wacouta, the last of the Red Wing chiefs, died. With no chief to accept the family talisman, the Red Wing Band merged with other Santee on the reservation.

This portrait of Red Wing is the artist's conception of the man. There are no known authenticated photographs of the Red Wing Chiefs mentioned in this book.

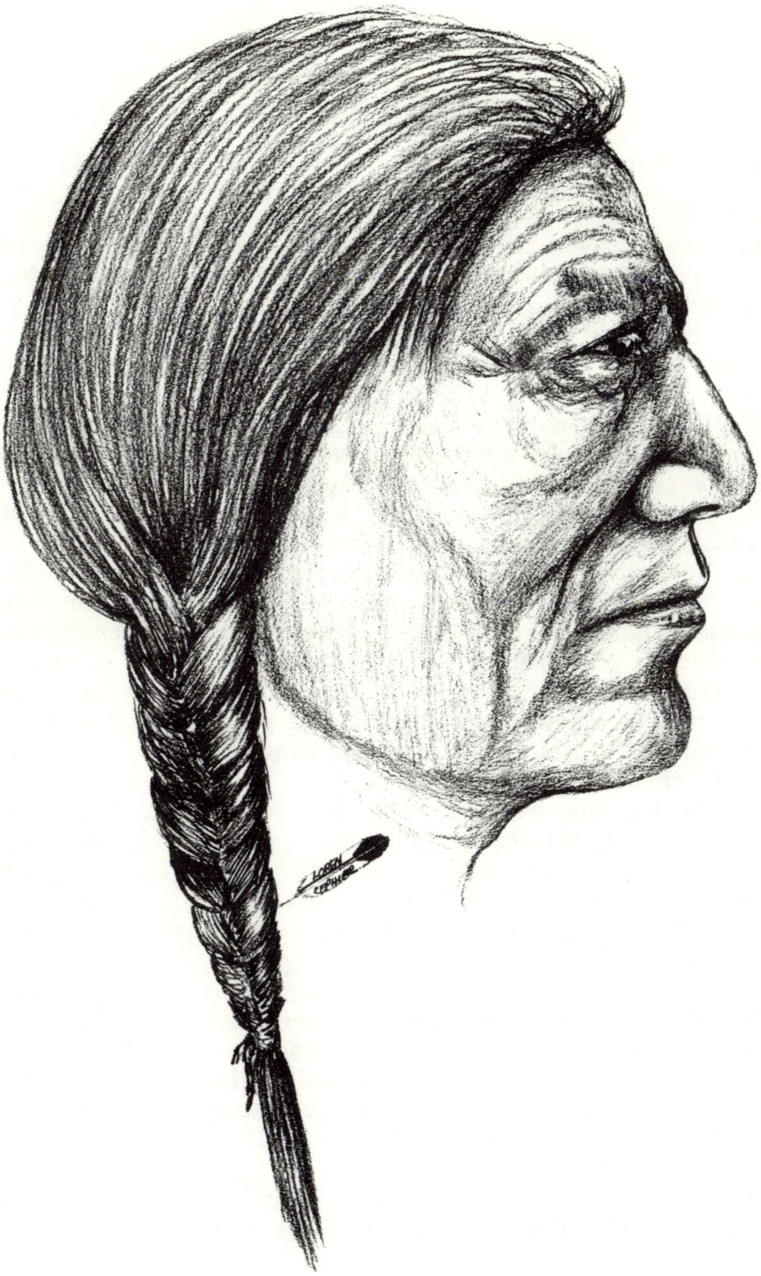

SHAKOPEE

Mdewakanton Santee

When the Sioux were first discovered during the 17th Century, the eastern bands were driven southward from their lands, the region near Lake Superior, by the hostile Objibwa (Chippewa). The French fur traders and settlers called SHAKOPEE I, LE DEMI DOUZEN, which probably means in corrupted Old French, "The Half Dozen". Shakopee I was known to have fought against the Chippewa in the Elm River Battle in 1772.

SHAKOPEE II first entered historical records by his presence at the signing of the first treaty between the United States and the Sioux Nation in 1805. Seven years later, Shakopee II fought with the British in the War of 1812 against the relatively new country, the United States of America. But after the war, Shakopee II became loyal to America.

He was a man who struck different persons differently. Major Forsyth, who visited Shakopee II's village in 1819, did not like him describing him as being blustering and rude. However, the missionary in the area at the time, S. W. Pond, Jr., thought this Shakopee II to be a man of marked ability. Shakopee II was an orator with an impressive speaking voice. He used this power effectively, often putting his thoughts into eloquent pointed statements. His statements were quoted by other Santee and taught to their children.

Settling about a mile west of the Red Wood River in Minnesota in 1852, Shakopee befriended the white people and kept his band within the terms of the 1851 Treaty while waiting for the government to meet its promises. Had he not died during the summer of 1862, just before the Santee Uprising, Shakopee II would have continued to counsel the Santee for peace.

Shakopee II was succeeded by his son, EATOKA. Although Eatoka assumed the name of his father, Shakopee, he lacked his father's intelligence and leadership qualities. The actual leader of the Shakopee Band during the fighting of 1862 was the dead chief's brother, Hochokaduta. Hochokaduta hated whites. Defeated at the Battle of Wood Lake on September 23, 1862, Hochokaduta, Shakopee III and their band fled northward with Little Crow to Canada.

Hochokaduta was killed by the Chippewa during the winter of 1863. Shakopee III was captured by the United States Army and hung at Fort Snelling in 1864.

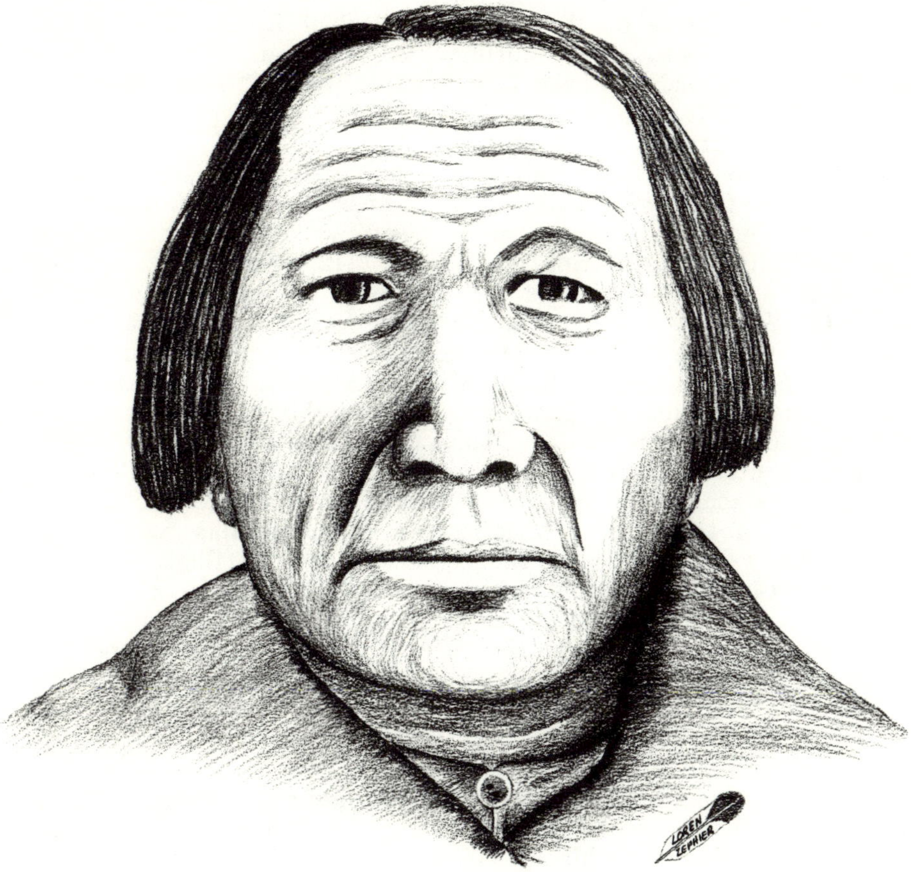
LOREN ZEPHIER

TAMAHA

1775-1860

Wahpeton or Mdewakanton Santee

Known to the French as "The One-Eyed Sioux", Tamaha and his people made their home on the Upper Mississippi River. Tamaha did have only one eye, losing an eye during a lacrosse game during his boyhood. His Indian name has been translated to mean "Rising Moon" or "Rising Elk".

Tamaha was present at the signing of Pike's $2,000 (the reputed price of 60 gallons of whiskey and several hundreds of dollars worth of trade goods) Treaty of 1805. This was the first between the U. S. Government and the Sioux people. As one of the few Santee who remained loyal to the United States during the War of 1812, Tamaha accompanied Manuel Lisa up the Missouri River to the mouth of the James River to influence the Santee not to fight against the Americans. He continued his journey from there to Prairie du Chien where he was arrested by the British. The British hoping for information on American activities on the frontier imprisoned Tamaha. Tamaha revealed nothing. Later that year after being released by the British, Tamaha returned to the Upper Mississippi for the winter. The next spring, he returned to Prairie du Chien as the British were abandoning the fort and setting fire to several buildings. On top of one of the burning buildings an American flag was flying. Tamaha daringly dashed into the flames and rescued the flag.

Governor Clark in St. Louis richly rewarded Tamaha for his loyalty and patriotic act to the United States by giving him a captain's uniform with stovepipe hat and a meaningless title. The chief treasured the uniform and hat as long as he lived, wearing them only on special occasions.

Governor Clark commissioned Chief Tamaha, an already recognized Santee chief, as "head chief" of all the Dakota people. This empty title was never recognized by any other tribe.

Tamaha's extreme loyalty to the United States was partially induced by his fondness for the white man's whiskey. The American representatives freely gave Tamaha whiskey. What once encouraged him onward to his glory also led him to a pathetic end. In his old age he relived the glory of his patriotic deeds by telling and retelling of his brave deeds against the British. He loved to show off his gifts from Governor Clark and became a tragic mockery of his former self. He died on the reservation near Wabasha, Minnesota in 1860.

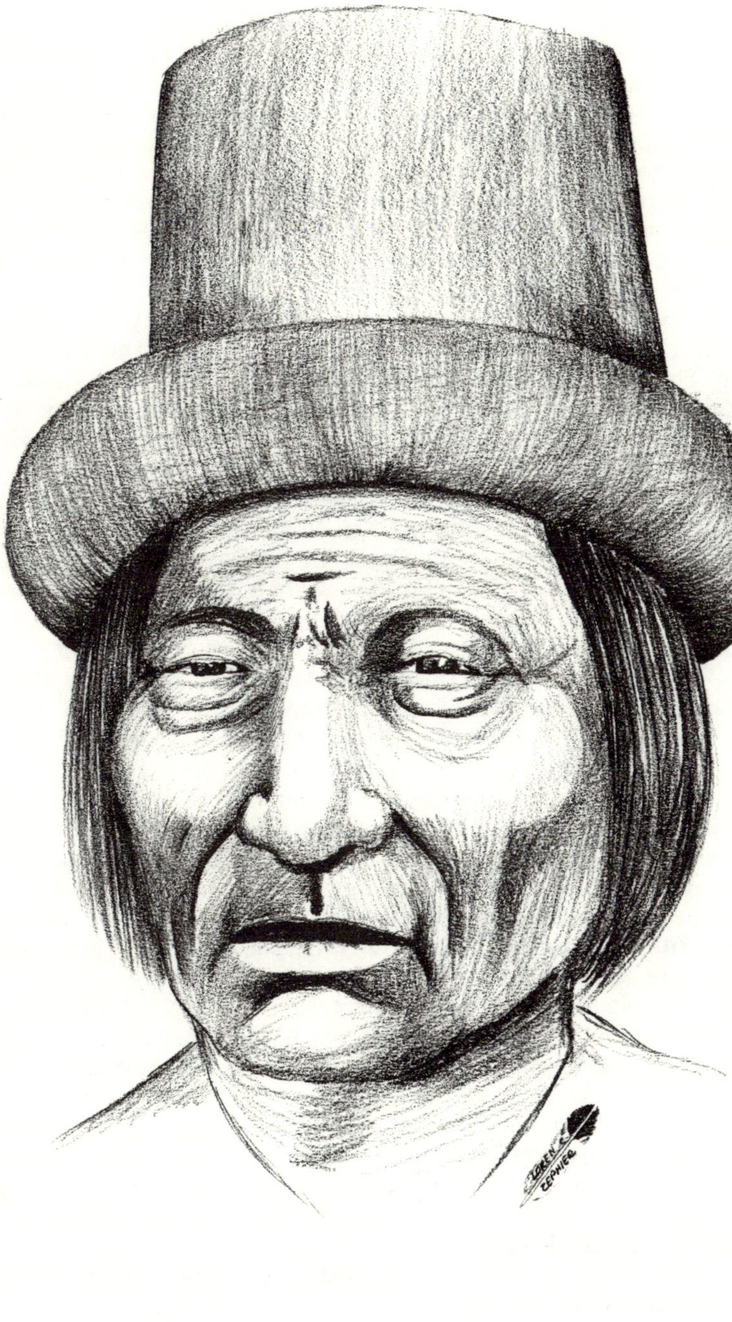

APADANI, STRUCK BY THE REE

1804-1881

Yankton

One Sioux legend tells of a Yankton baby boy born about September 1, 1804 who was "christened" by being wrapped in an American flag. The white men who wrapped the Indian child in the United States stars and stripes were Captains Meriwether Lewis and William Clark on their famous expedition to the Pacific Coast by way of the Missouri River. Lewis and Clark were meeting with the Yankton tribe at Calument Bluff on the Missouri River when Apadani, Struck By The Ree, was born. They predicted that the baby would become a great leader of his people and a steadfast friend to the whites.

Whether the legend is true or not, Struck By The Ree took pride in his loyalty to the United States and always cooperated with the whites.

Struck By The Ree's village was at the present site of Yankton, South Dakota, but his band ranged freely between the Sioux and Missouri Rivers. As the demand by white settlers for more land grew louder, the government bargained with the tribes. The Treaty of 1858 gave up all the old Yankton hunting grounds between the Sioux and Missouri Rivers to white settlement in exchange for a 400,000 acre reservation on the Missouri River, above Choteau Creek in present day Charles-Mix County, South Dakota. Struck By The Ree signed the treaty and used his influence to prevent a Yankton uprising by those who opposed the treaty. The Santee uprising in Minnesota followed four years later.

Struck By The Ree, living on the reservation, abided by the treaty terms during the bloody year of 1862 and he successfully kept the Yankton out of the war. But he also went one step further—he warned many white settlers of their danger.

Educating Indian children in white man's schools was at first strongly opposed by Struck By The Ree. He felt, as many Sioux leaders did, that their children would forget their Indian ways. After the Indian agent of the reservation showed him that he had agreed to white man's way of education when he signed the 1858 Treaty, Struck By The Ree reversed his opinion. He fully cooperated with the treaty's terms by personally seeing to it that the schools were filled.

Legend has also clouded the truth behind this Yankton chief's name. There are two versions as to how he earned his name. One tells that as a young man he was beaten in personal combat with an Arikara (Ree) warrior. The Ree partially scalped the Yankton who wore a kerchief or hat the rest of his life to hide the scar. For this he was called "Struck By The Ree". The second legend reversed the roles—the young Yankton spearing the Ree killing him—and thus he was known as "Strike the Ree". Even the spelling of his native name has three versions—APADANI, PADANIAPAPI or PALANEAPE.

During his last years legend was forgotten and the Yankton chief was kindly known as "Old Strike".

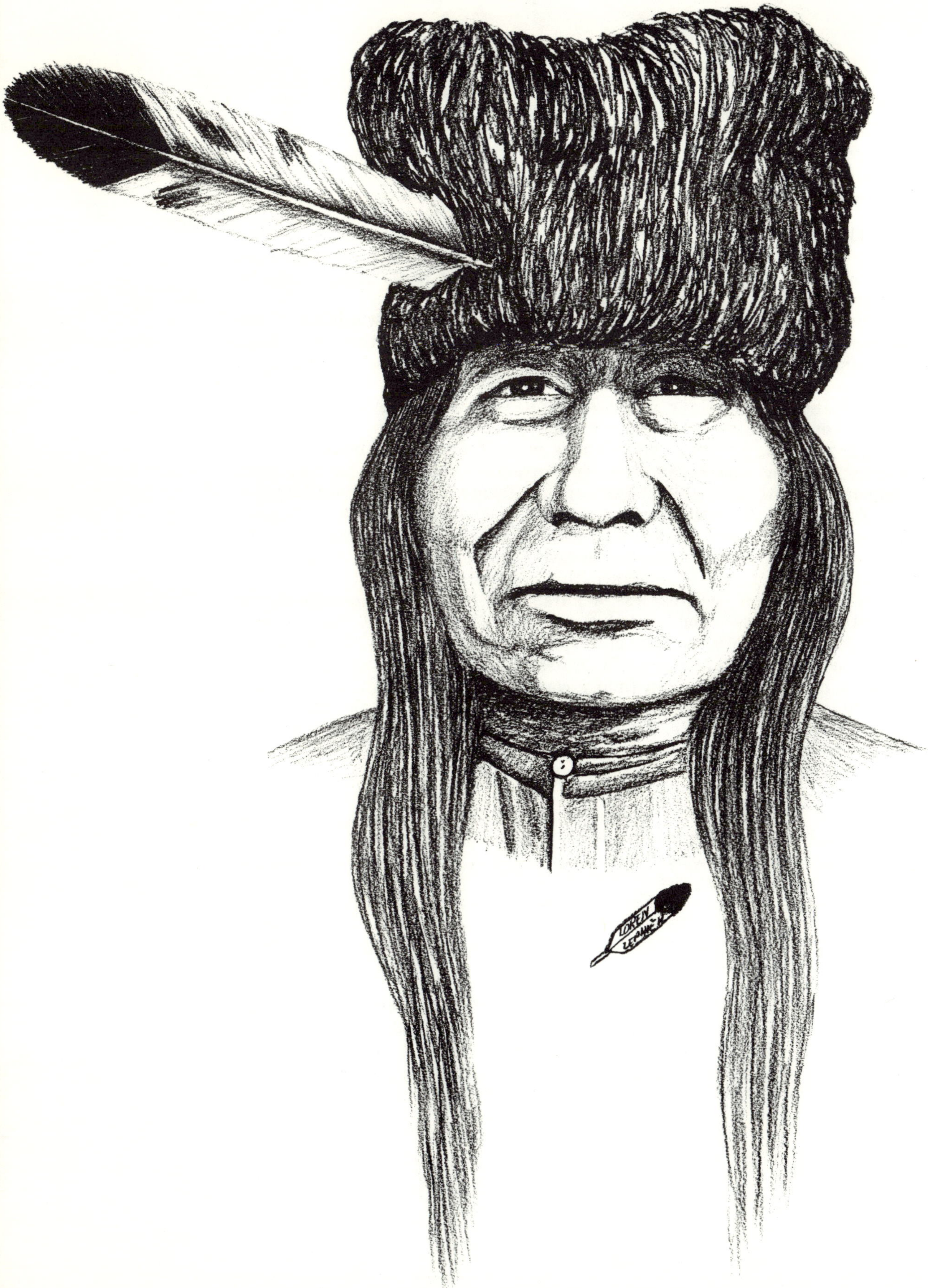

TAOYA TE DUTA, LITTLE CROW

1823(?)-1863

Mdewakanton Santee

The name LITTLE CROW was given to four generations of Santee chiefs. The first fought with the British in Canada during the American Revolutionary War, 1776. TAOYA TE DUTA, "His Red People," was the fourth and best known of the Little Crow chiefs.

Sources disagree on the date of the fourth Little Crow's birth. Some sources record the dates as 1818, others state 1823. A third and final group state he was 60 years old at the time of the Minnesota Uprising in 1862.

By 1862, Little Crow and his people were settled near the Lower Agency on the Minnesota Reservation. He wore trousers and a brass-buttoned jacket, adopting white man's way of dress. He built a house, started farming and became an Episcopalian. For years he had been cooperating with the whites, keeping the treaty terms and waiting for the fulfillment of government promises. Discouraged and discontented, Little Crow lost much of his influence over the tribe by trying to live as a white man. Many of the conservative traditional Santee accused him of betraying them when he signed the treaties.

The winter of 1861-62 was a harsh and bitter time, especially for the starving Santee who waited for promised government rations that never came. Little Crow lost more prestige and power with his people when he failed to talk Agent Galbraith into giving the hungry Santee food. When the summer sun finally warmed the land again, a delegation of Santee leaders visited Little Crow. Unable to withstand the charges of cowardice from his people, Little Crow agreed to lead his people against the white settlers and soldiers. Although he did agree to fight, Little Crow hesitated because he understood the military superiority of the whites.

Little Crow directed the Santee during the Uprising until he was disastrously defeated at the Battle of Wood Lake on September 23, 1862. Little Crow and his people then turned and fled to Canada and safety by way of the Dakota prairies.

In June of 1863 Little Crow, his son, Woinapa, and a few followers returned to Minnesota near Hutchinson to obtain horses. They wanted the horses to help them adjust to the nomadic life now forced upon them. (The Santee had been the most sedimentary of all the Sioux.) They were discovered, and on June 3, 1863, Little Crow was killed.

His body was thrown on an entrail heap of a slaughter house. Later his skeleton was removed and placed on display by the Minnesota State Historical Society. It wasn't until September 27, 1971, after his descendents completed years of negotiations, that Little Crow's remains were buried in the Santee cemetery north of Flandreau, South Dakota.

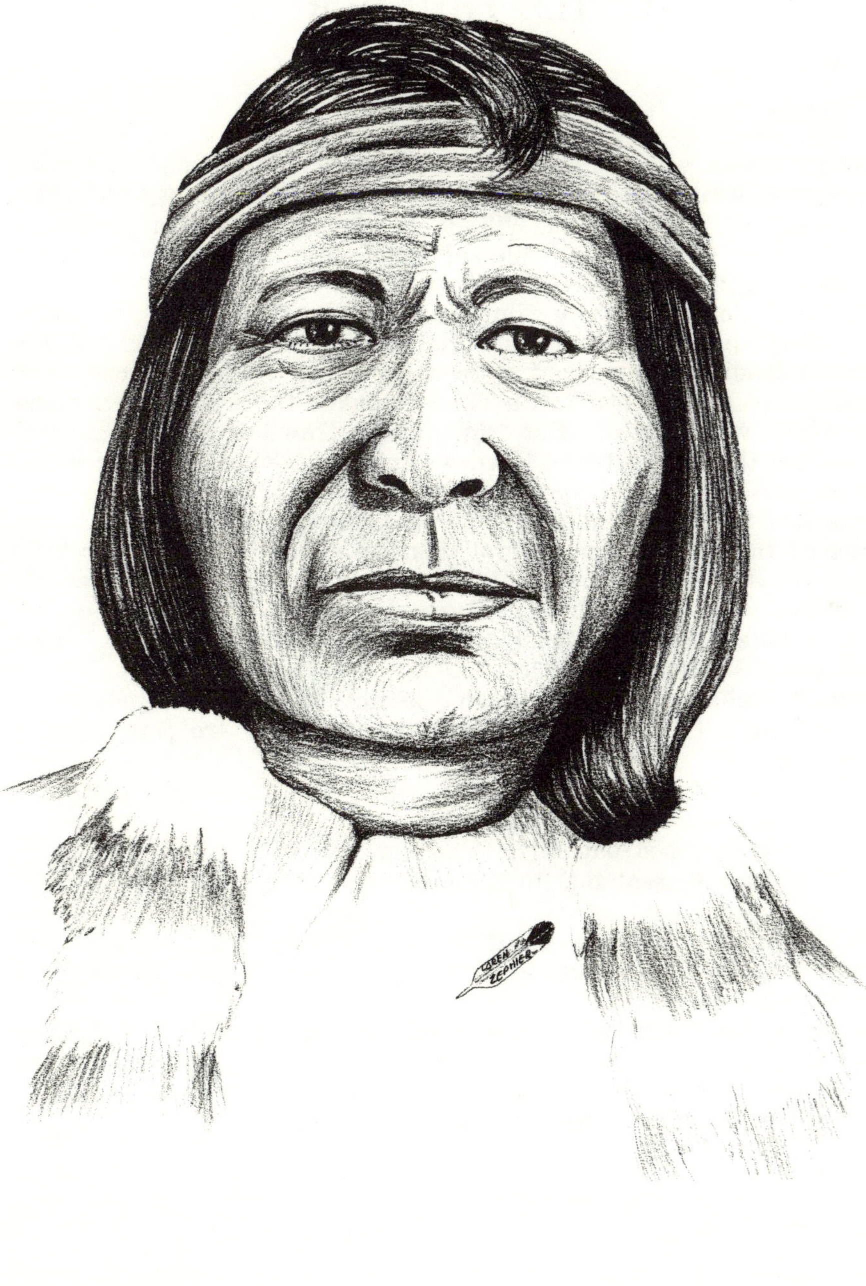

LITTLE THUNDER

(?)-1879

Brule Teton

Little Thunder was the leader of a wild and warlike band of Brules who harrassed white emigrants along the Overland Trail to California. In the spring of 1855 General William S. Harney headed a campaign against the Sioux to teach the Brule and Oglala a lesson they would never forget, thus letting the whites travel in peace.

At Ash Hollow, a favorite campsite of wagon trains near the forks of the Platte River in what is now Nebraska, Little Thunder and his Brules were holding an emigrant train under seige. General Harney and 400-some troops arrived and Little Thunder asked for a council with the general which was granted. But while Little Thunder and the general spoke beneath the flag of truce, Harney's troops deployed themselves, according to previous orders, to ambush the Brules. When all was ready, Harney ended the council abruptly telling Little Thunder his intentions of killing all the Brules. The general then permitted the chief to return to his people. As he raced towards his people, Little Thunder signaled his people to flee. They ran right into Harney's cavalry. Overwhelmed, 136 Brules were killed; the entire Brule camp was captured; and yet the Brules wounded many soldiers, killing 13.

General William S. Harney became known to the plains Indians as WHITE BEARD, THE BUTCHER, even as the army troopers proudly sang the song:

> We did not make a blunder
> We rubbed out Little Thunder
> And we sent him to the other side of Jordan.

Little Thunder was not killed at Ash Hollow. He gathered the remnants of his band and lived thereafter in a fearful peace. Harney had taught him his lesson.

Although the Corn and Loafer bands at the Spotted Tail Agency on the old Missouri Ponca Agency were considered progressive by the whites, they were held in contempt by the Indians. Little Thunder finally settled with these bands where he died about 1879.

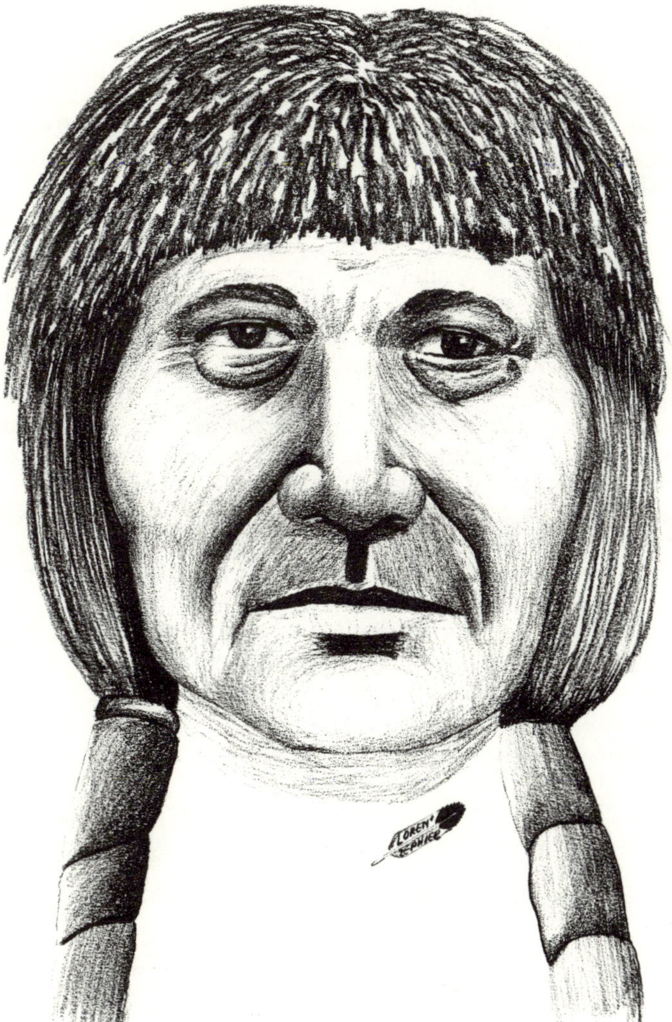

INKPADUTA

1815-1882

Wahpekute Santee

The renegade band of Wahpekute Santee led by Inkpaduta saw its beginning when Wamdesapa, Inkpaduta's father, killed his old rival, Chief Tasagi. Wamdesapa died in 1848 leaving his son to direct the freely roaming band of renegades. They roamed the prairies of South Dakota, Iowa and Minnesota. Other members of the Wahpekutes wanted no part of the fierce, cruel leader whose band became a refuge for cast-outs and undesirables from many Santee tribes.

Inkpaduta's extreme hatred for whites seemed to be derived from the senseless murdering in 1854 of his brother and family by Henry Lott. Henry Lott, a white whiskey trader and horse thief, reputedly had killed without cause. For this reason, probably, Inkpaduta fiercely opposed white encroachment on the Minnesota frontier. He did not sign one of the 1851 treaties, but often appeared at the agencies demanding a share of the annuity payments.

During the severe winter of 1856-57, even the agency Santee suffered. Inkpaduta's band, with no annuities to fall back on, survived only by begging and preying on white settlements. A white posse, angered over the shooting of a dog which had bitten a member, forcibly took their weapons leaving them unable to even hunt. The weapons were recovered in some manner. The Inkpaduta band then proceeded to retaliate against the whites by a general slaughter of settlers in the area.

On March 8 and 9, 1856, Inkpaduta led his band on a murdering spree that ended with 35 deaths and the capture of 4 women in the Okoboji and Spirit Lakes area in Iowa. These deaths have been recorded in history as the Spirit Lake Massacre.

Inkpaduta showed no mercy to the captive white women. Two of the women died after the band fled into what is now South Dakota. Mrs. Margaret Ann Marble and Abbie Gardner were rescued by other Santee for the promise of individual rewards and the return of the entire tribe's annuities. The Santee hotly resented being deprived of their annuities for the actions of the 14 or 15 members of Inkpaduta's band of Wahpekute Santee.

A little more than 5 years later during the Minnesota Uprising, Inkpaduta was one of the ingenious leaders at the battles of Big Mound and White Stone Hill, 1863. It was a young member of Inkpaduta's band who shot Dr. Joseph S. Weiser that started the Big Mound Battle (Page 20). Inkpaduta led his small band up and down the frontier killing settlers and leaving a trail of terror. The whites blamed all of the Santee for his actions.

At the Battle of the Little Big Horn, Inkpaduta was one of the few Santee present. Afterwards, fled into Canada never making peace with the whites. He died in 1882.

This portrait of Inkpaduta is the artist's conception of the man. There are no known authenticated photographs of Inkpaduta.

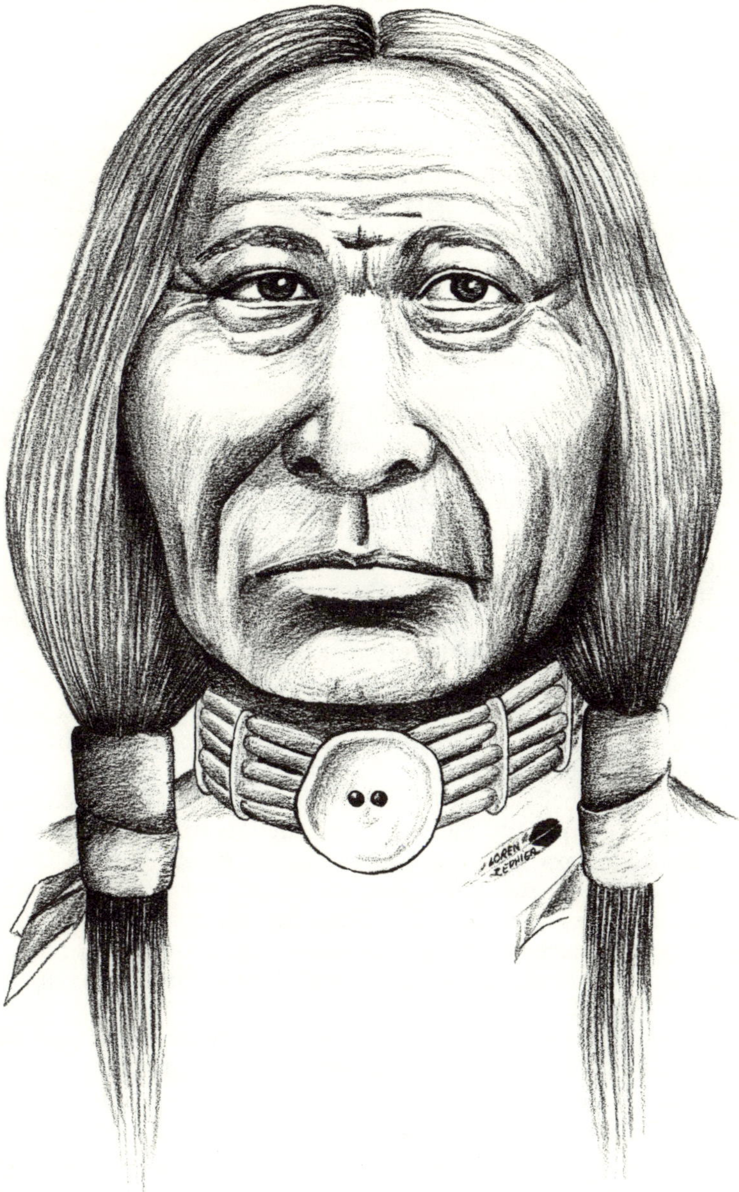
LOREN
ZEPHIER

WAANATAN, MARTIN CHARGER
1833-1900

Two Kettle Teton

Charger was the son of Turkey Head whose Two Kettle mother claimed that Captain Meriwether Lewis was the father of her son. The Two Kettle were visited by the 1804 Lewis and Clark expedition at the mouth of the Bad River. The Indians recalled that some of their young women had lain with the white men.

Charger was given the boyhood name of WOWACINYE, "Dependable, because he was an obedient and patient child." He was a skilled hunter by the time he was in his teens and went on his first battle when he was eighteen.

As a young adult, Charger and his lifelong friend, Kills Game And Comes Back, formed a new society based on nonviolence and unselfish sharing with the less fortunate. The tenets of nonviolence of the new society were so out of character with the Teton warrior culture that the young men were ridiculed and called "foolish" and came to be known as the Fool Soldiers.

In November of 1862, a fugitive Santee band, led by White Lodge, fleeing the retribution white soldiers were taking against the participants of the Minnesota Uprising, sought refuge among the Teton. With them were white captives of the August 20, 1862, Lake Shetek Massacre (Minnesota). The captives were Mrs. Laura (William) Duley, two of the Duley children, Mrs. Julia (John) Wright, her daughter Dora Wright, Lillian Everett, Rosanna and Ella Ireland.

Charger and the Fool Soldiers voluntarily went to the rescue of the captives and were again made fun of and called traitors by their tribe. Charger and his followers effected the rescue at a site across the river from the mouth of the Grand River and used their own horses, blankets, and guns in exchange for the captives. They had only a few blankets, one gun, and one horse to carry the captives safely back to Fort Pierre with the whole rescue team enduring great hardship traveling in a November blizzard.

No record can be found of any repayment for the personal possessions of the Fool Soldier Band given in exchange for the captives.

Charger's camp became a refuge for destitute Sioux fleeing before General Sibley's campaign in 1863. After reservation settlement, Charger and his followers successfully adapted to the new life. He was baptized an Episcopalian in 1882 and worked the rest of his life for peace with the whites.

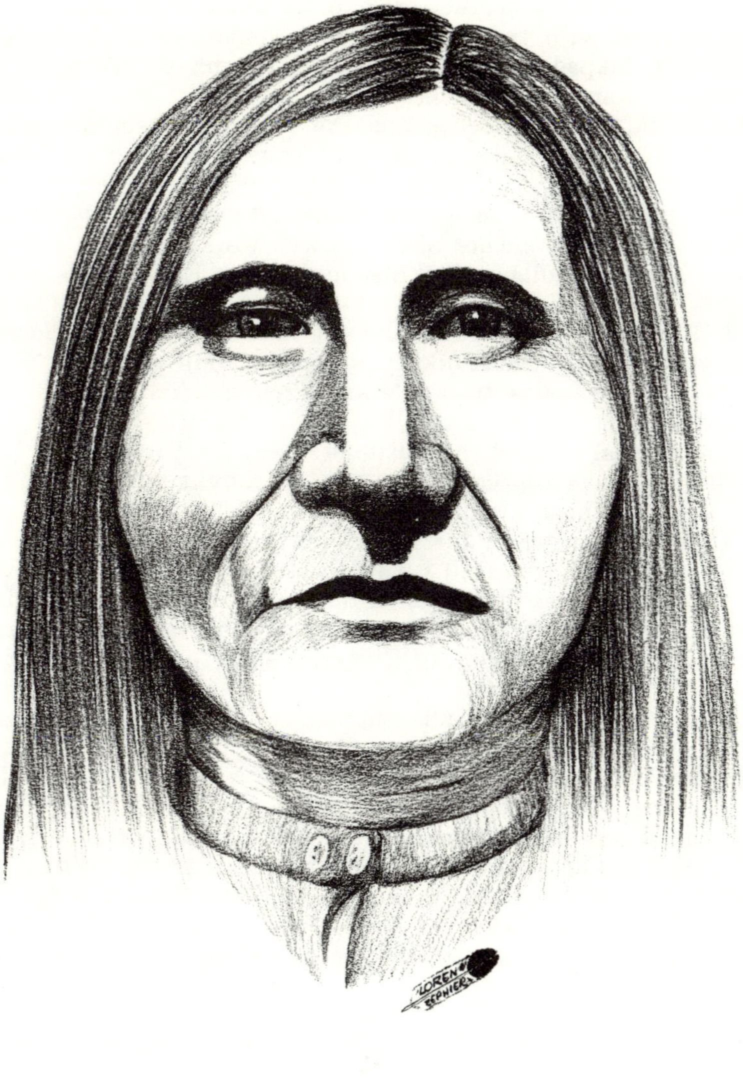

PIZI, GALL

1832-1896

Hunkpapa Teton

Gall who later became one of the leading warrior chiefs of the Teton was born near the Moreau River about 1832. Although he was orphaned as a young boy and raised by relatives, he distinguished himself during his early teens as a warrior and a hunter. A childhood attempt to eat the gall of an animal killed by a neighbor led to his name PIZI, Gall.

Gall was involved with the Battle of Big Mound, July 24, 1863. A young renegade of Inkpaduta's band shot Dr. Joseph S. Weiser, First Minnesota Mounted Rangers, on a large knoll in advance of the meeting site between General Sibley's troops and the friendly Sissetons east of Bismarck. With troopers retaliating on the entire gathering of Indians for the renegade's act, the Sioux turned and fled using all their military tactics to give time to the women and children to escape. The largest mortality rate was among the older Sissetons who were caught at the rear of the fleeing column of Indians. Gall also assisted in Red Cloud's war of 1866-68.

Sitting Bull was impressed with the young man's courage and adopted him as a younger brother. The Hunkpapas accepted Gall as Sitting Bull's lieutenant. He soon became a trusted warrior chief after leading them to many victories.

Gall was a principal chief at the Battle of the Little Big Horn in 1876. Although he did not have supreme authority, he fought with skill and a ferocity that inspired those around him. Much of his battle fierceness was derived from the murder of his family during Reno's first and only attack at the Little Big Horn. Gall turned back Reno's attack. Grieving and angered, Gall then turned hundreds of his warriors on a frontal attack against General George Armstrong Custer. After cooperating with Crazy Horse and Two Moon in annihiliating Custer, Gall returned to the siege of Reno and Benteen at the bluffs.

After the Little Big Horn, Gall followed Sitting Bull into Canada. But in 1881 he and Sitting Bull had a parting of ways. Gall returned to the United States leading a band of 300 Hunkpapas, almost immediately encountering General Miles' troopers under the command of Major Guido Ilges at the Poplar River in Montana. After a short battle with weakened warriors who had little ammunition to protect their starving women and children, Gall surrendered. They were held at Fort Buford until Gall pledged his loyalty and obedience to the United States.

He and his people were settled on the Standing Rock Reservation where he built a home at Oak Creek near the Wakpala. James McLaughlin, the Indian Agent of Standing Rock, described Gall as a large man of noble presence with military talents of high order plus a personal character that won respect from those in contact with him.

Gall remained peaceable on the reservation. He opposed the Treaty of 1889 and would not sign the agreement that broke up the great Sioux Reservation.

Gall took no part in in the Messiah Ghost Dance religion, but worked with his people to convince them that cooperation was the only recourse left. He died at his home on the Wakpala.

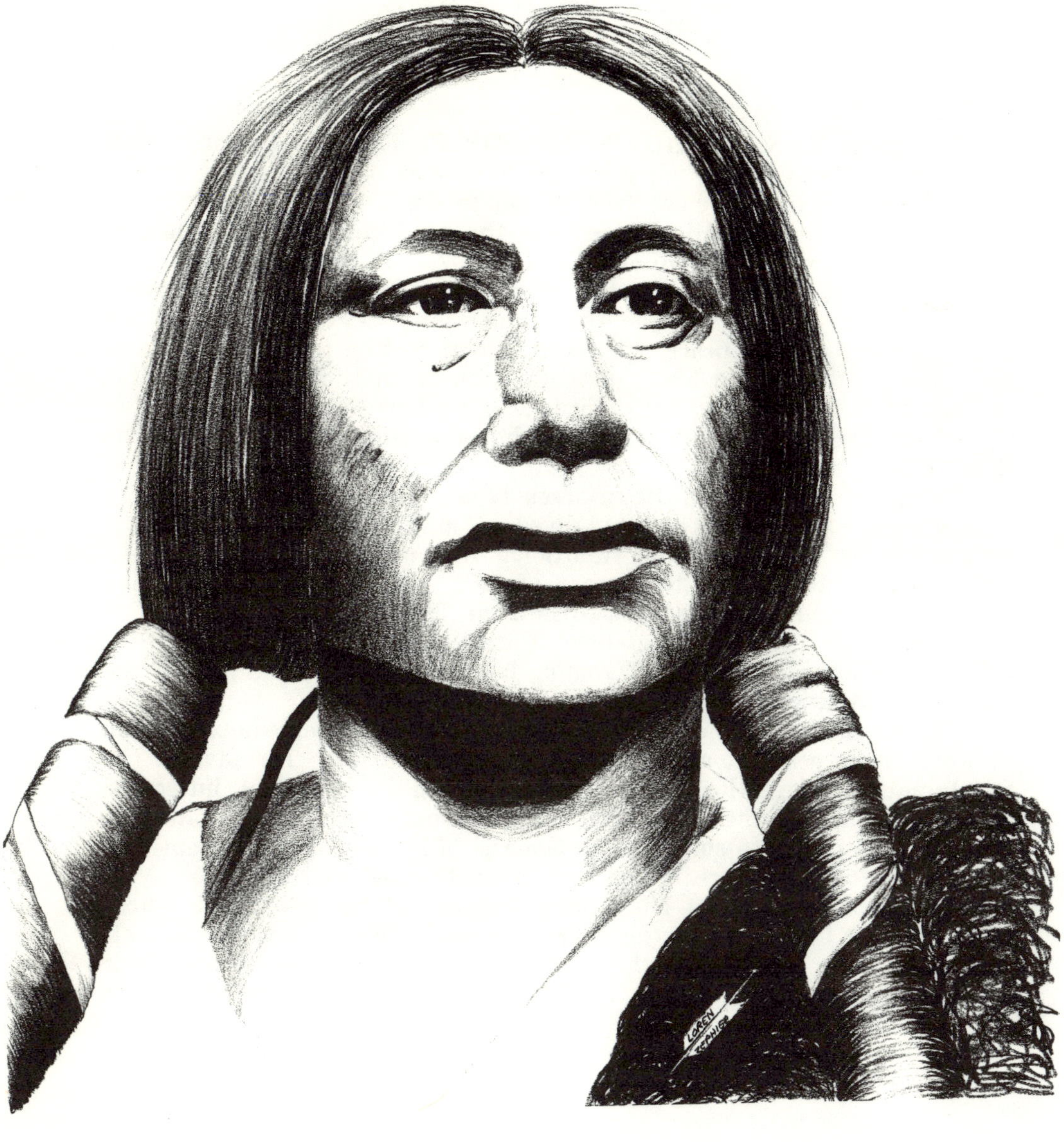

TASHUNKOPIPAPE, MAN AFRAID OF HIS HORSES

Oglala Teton

The name MAN AFRAID OF HIS HORSES is the inaccurate translation of the Teton phrase which means, "the man of whose horse we are afraid," and was handed down from father to son.

Old Man Afraid of His Horses was the head chief of the Oglala in 1854 and the leader of the Hunkpatila band. After the head chief's position was taken by Red Cloud, Old Man was called PAYABA, "Pushed Aside". He refused to sign the 1865 treaty but knew the power of the white men and wanted peace if it could be obtained on terms favorable to the Indians. It was Old Man's peaceful inclination that led the Oglalas to flock to Red Cloud who led them in war against the whites. Old Man signed the 1869 treaty but joined in the opposition to the sale of the Black Hills.

Young Man Afraid of His Horses became an active leader of the Oglala even while his father still lived. Young Man was considered a progressive as opposed to the traditional Indians and aided Agent McGillycuddy in attempting to dispose of Red Cloud. However, he sided with the older chiefs and refused to sign the Treaty of 1889.

During the height of the Ghost Dance craze Young Man left Pine Ridge on an extended hunt in Wyoming because he wanted no part of the dangerous situation.

He returned after the Wounded Knee disaster and immediately began to work for a peaceful settlement of the whole affair. He advised the Oglala not to avenge the deaths at Wounded Knee for if they did so the soldiers would kill them all. He visited Ghost Dance camps and encouraged the people to surrender to General Miles and assured them that they would be kindly treated if they gave themselves up.

Young Man Afraid of His Horses was one of the few Teton whose spirit was not broken by the disaster at Wounded Knee. Both he and his father had long known that the white men were fickle in keeping their word, but they also knew that the Sioux could never again be victorious.

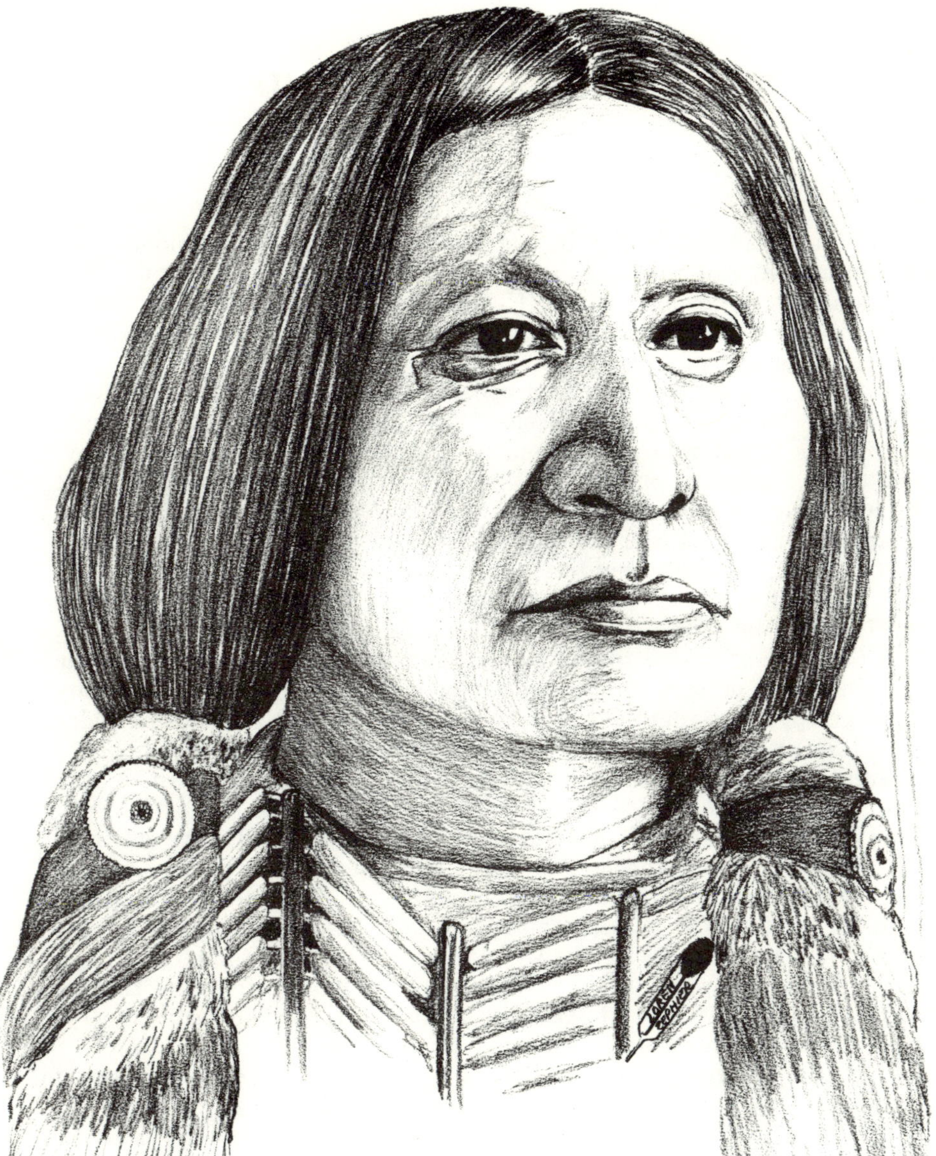

MAHPIALUTA, RED CLOUD

1822(?)-1909

Oglala Teton

Red Cloud was the leader of his mother's Oglala Old Smoke band later becoming chief of the Bad Faces Band. His father was a Brule. Red Cloud was a shrewd observer of the United States Army's military tactics and used the same in his battles. He opposed white encroachment and was an influential leader of the Teton Sioux.

Red Cloud refused to sign the proposed treaty of 1865 at Fort Pierre which would have given permission for the government to build a road through the Powder River country. When the road was built anyway and forts erected to protect the white travelers, Red Cloud began his war to force the whites to leave. For two years, 1866-1868, he engaged in sporadic battles with the United States that in effect kept the road and forts closed. Finally the forts and road were abandoned and Red Cloud, thinking the whites would now keep their word, signed the treaty at Fort Laramie in 1868.

Red Cloud then moved to the agency which bore his name and made every attempt to convince the Oglala to honor the treaty. He made many trips to Washington to intercede in behalf of his people. He and other older traditional Sioux leaders refused to sign the Treaty of 1889 which broke up the great Sioux Reservation that Red Cloud had fought so hard to gain in 1868.

Pine Ridge Agent V. T. McGillycuddy and Red Cloud were enemies of long standing. They fueded for years and Red Cloud petitioned the Interior Department many times to have the agent removed. McGillycuddy in turn attempted to destroy Red Cloud's traditional power by appointing others head chiefs of the Oglala. However, Red Cloud, although old and nearly blind, remained a respected leader with influential friends in Washington and retained his power. At last, after seven years of trying, Red Cloud saw his enemy removed from office.

Red Cloud became a Roman Catholic, but still gave tacit support and sympathy to the Ghost Dance religion. After the massacre at Wounded Knee, Red Cloud yielded to the inevitable and quietly retired, but remained opposed to civilization until his death.

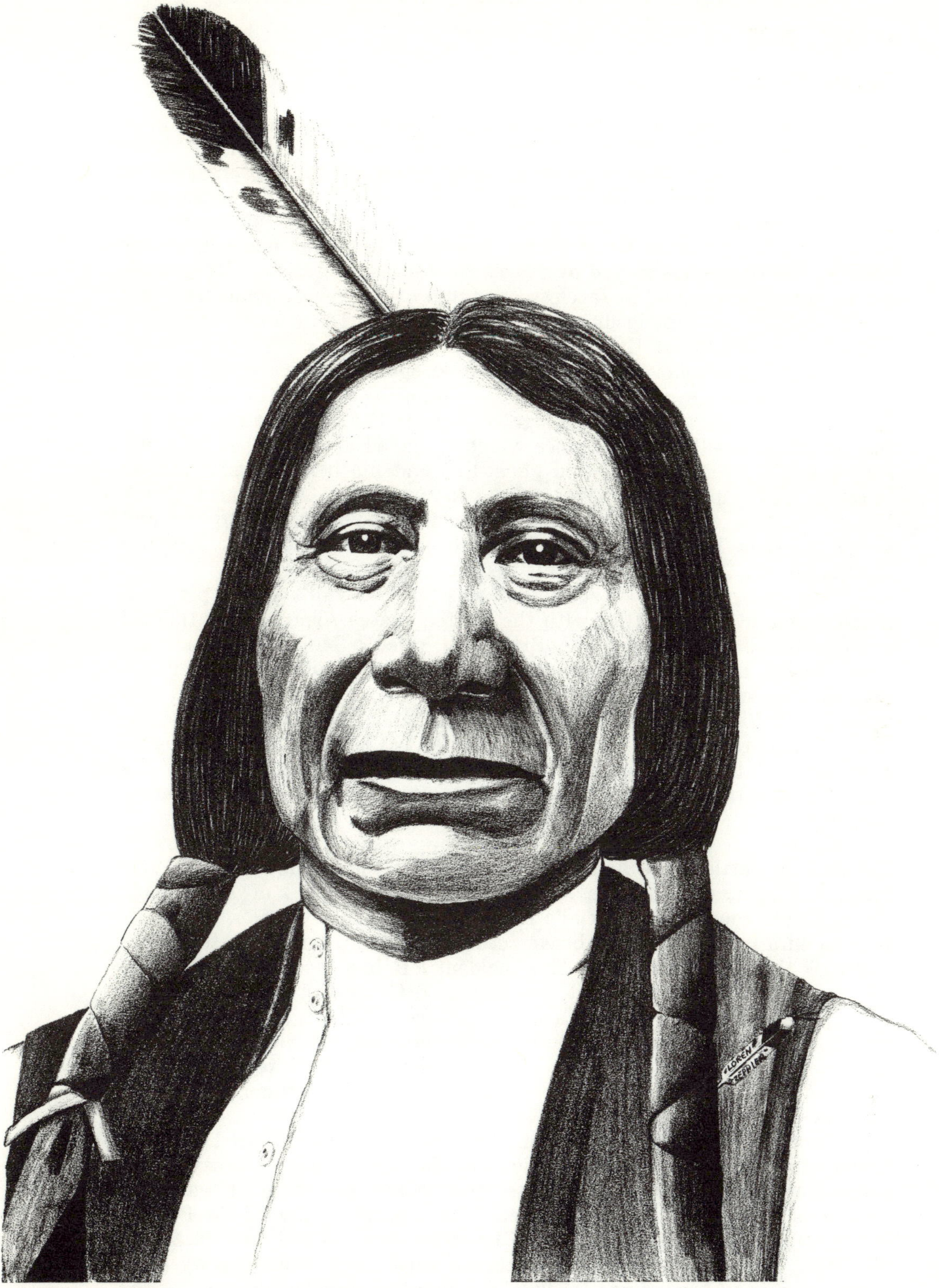

TASHUNKA WITCO, CRAZY HORSE

1840(?)-1877

Oglala Teton

Although Crazy Horse died in 1877, he still is held as a sacred figure to the modern Sioux Nation. Little is known of Crazy Horse's early years except that he was born near Rapid Creek on the eastern side of the Black Hills about 1840. One legend describes Crazy Horse as very light-skinned with soft light-colored hair. There is no authenticated sketch or photograph of Crazy Horse (contrary to claims made in recent years). His image has sacred overtures for the modern Sioux. They wish his image to be cloaked in faceless anonymity to forever symbolize their defeat and the need for inspired leaders once more. To honor their wishes there is no portrait of Crazy Horse in this work.

Crazy Horse believed that he possessed special powers given to him by WAKANTANKA, the Great Spirit. To him, the men of the earth were living in the shadow of the real, perfect world. Crazy Horse reached the real world by a self-induced trance which he called dreaming. In this, his sacred world, everything floated ghost-like and his horse always danced in a wild, crazy manner. This was his vision and it led to his name, Crazy Horse. (Before every battle Crazy Horse dreamed himself into the real world to renew his courage and ability to endure intense pain. Because of this power, Crazy Horse led his people to many victories.)

This young Oglala, whose mother was Spotted Tail's sister, played a decisive role in many battles with the United States Army. He witnessed the Grattan Battle of 1854. (A Brule had killed a Mormon's wandering cow. Second Lieutenant J. L. Grattan, through a drunk interpreter, demanded the surrender of the guilty warrior. Grattan then opened fire upon the Indians. The Sioux killed Grattan and his troopers, but their chief, Conquering Bear, was fatally wounded.) Crazy Horse never again fully trusted nor expected the white men to keep their promises. He signed no treaties, hated the ways of the white men and spurned reservation life.

By the time of his mid-teens Crazy Horse was a full-fledged warrior. His skill in battle made him much admired by the members in his own band, but aroused jealousies in another, the Bad Faces of Red Cloud. Crazy Horse courted Red Cloud's niece, Black Buffalo Woman, but while he was on a raid a Bad Face brave returned to camp fending a toothache and took the girl as his wife. This incident left bad feelings between the two men and their friends that survived until Crazy Horse's death.

Crazy Horse later married a woman of the Northern Cheyenne. With this marriage he soon became the leader of the Southern Sioux and Northern Cheyenne who refused reservation life and any of white man's ways. He frequently attacked soldiers, defeating Colonel Fetterman and his 80 men on December 21, 1866.

Then the War Department of the United States declared that all tribes must be located on reservations by January 1, 1876. Crazy Horse ignored the declaration and was the first to feel the sting of war. His village of more than 100 lodges near the mouth of the Little Powder River was destroyed by Colonel J. J. Reynolds and his 450 men on March 17, 1876. As Reynolds and his men turned with Crazy Horse's pony herd, Crazy Horse and his Indians followed for 20 miles recapturing most of the horses.

On June 17, 1876, with his band swollen to more than 1,200 Oglalas and Cheyennes, Crazy Horse defeated General Crook at the Battle of the Rosebud. Even Red Cloud's son had joined Crazy Horse's band. Crazy Horse then moved north to join Sitting Bull at the Little Big Horn. He was an important strategic commander in the fight against Custer. After the victory at the Little Big Horn, Crazy Horse harrassed General Crook's pursuing forces by fighting only at the time and place of his own choosing.

Crazy Horse, who refused to go to the reservation or flee to Canada as other Indian refugees were doing, set up winter camp in the Wolf Mountains. On January 8, 1877, with two pieces of artillery and a force of a few men, Colonel Nelson A. Miles attacked the Wolf Mountain village. Miles destroyed the village, but Crazy Horse led his people away in good order. With nearly no supplies, these people held out for another four months.

General Crook then turned to new tactics. First he convinced Spotted Tail to go to Crazy Horse to convince him to surrender, but Crazy Horse would not meet with his uncle. Red Cloud was then sent by Crook with the general's promise that Crazy Horse would have a reservation in his beloved Powder River country if he would come in. This promise and the fact that 1,100 men, women and children were starving, out of ammunition and with weak horses, persuaded Crazy Horse to give himself up at Fort Robinson on May 7, 1877.

Crazy Horse lived quietly at the fort until Crook heard rumors that the warrior chief was planning to break out. The old jealousies between Red Cloud's Bad Faces and Crazy Horse's followers came boiling to the surface. It appears that Red Cloud and his followers were jealous of the attention paid to Crazy Horse and plotted to be rid of him. Crazy Horse was arrested to prevent his rumored breakout of the reservation. As soon as he realized he was to be imprisoned, Crazy Horse drew his knife intent on fighting his way to freedom. He was grabbed from behind by his once close friend, Little Big Man, and during the following fight was bayoneted by a soldier.

Crazy Horse's death did not come swiftly as he would have liked in battle, but in lingering pain and delirium until the late night of September 5, 1877. His body was buried in secret by his parents.

More than a month later, the Indians of Red Cloud's and Spotted Tail's Agencies began their journey to the Missouri River. In one of the columns were Crazy Horse's people. While still some distance east of their new agency, Crazy Horse's people turned northward and fled towards Canada and freedom. The cavalry were too few to stop the rush towards Sitting Bull's exile camp. Crazy Horse's people carried with them the spirit of Crazy Horse—all that was left them.

TATANKA YOTANKA, SITTING BULL
1831 or 38-1890
Hunkpapa Teton

Sitting Bull, often erroneously called a chief, was a medicine man of great pyschic powers. He was influential over all of the Sioux as a prophet and orator who was able to sway even the white men with his eloquence.

On the way to the encampment at the Little Big Horn, Sitting Bull participated in the Sun Dance, fell into a trance in which he had a vision of soldiers falling from the sky as a gift from Wakantanka. His vision was fulfilled in the Custer battle.

After the Little Big Horn victory, Sitting Bull led his band into the Yellow Stone country to hunt. He was through fighting and wanted to be left alone. Later, after being constantly hounded by the U. S. Army, he fled to Canada. After four hungry years in the "grandmother's" land he returned to the United States on July 19, 1881.

Sitting Bull was then taken prisoner and confined at Fort Randall and later sent to the Standing Rock Reservation. His home became a haven for orphaned children and again he desired only to be left alone. However, officials believed that Sitting Bull's popularity with the frequent visits of many Sioux to his home hampered the progress of civilization. When Buffalo Bill Cody requested the Indian Bureau's permission for Sitting Bull to join his Wild West Show, it was readily given to remove the medicine man and his troublesome influence.

On his return to the reservation Sitting Bull supported the Ghost Dance movement and permitted the dance to be done at his Standing Rock camp. His involvement in the new religion alarmed agency personnel who feared Sitting Bull would lead an uprising.

On December 15, 1890, a troop of Indian police, commanded by Lieutenant Bull Head, was sent to arrest Sitting Bull. One of Sitting Bull's followers, Catch The Bear, protested the arrest, drew a gun and shot Bull Head. Bull Head turned and shot Sitting Bull who was also shot in the head by Red Tomahawk, another policeman. Some say Sitting Bull's son, Crow Foot, protested the arrest that started the shooting.

After their leader's death many of Sitting Bull's followers fled to the Cheyenne River Reservation to seek refuge with Chief Big Foot.

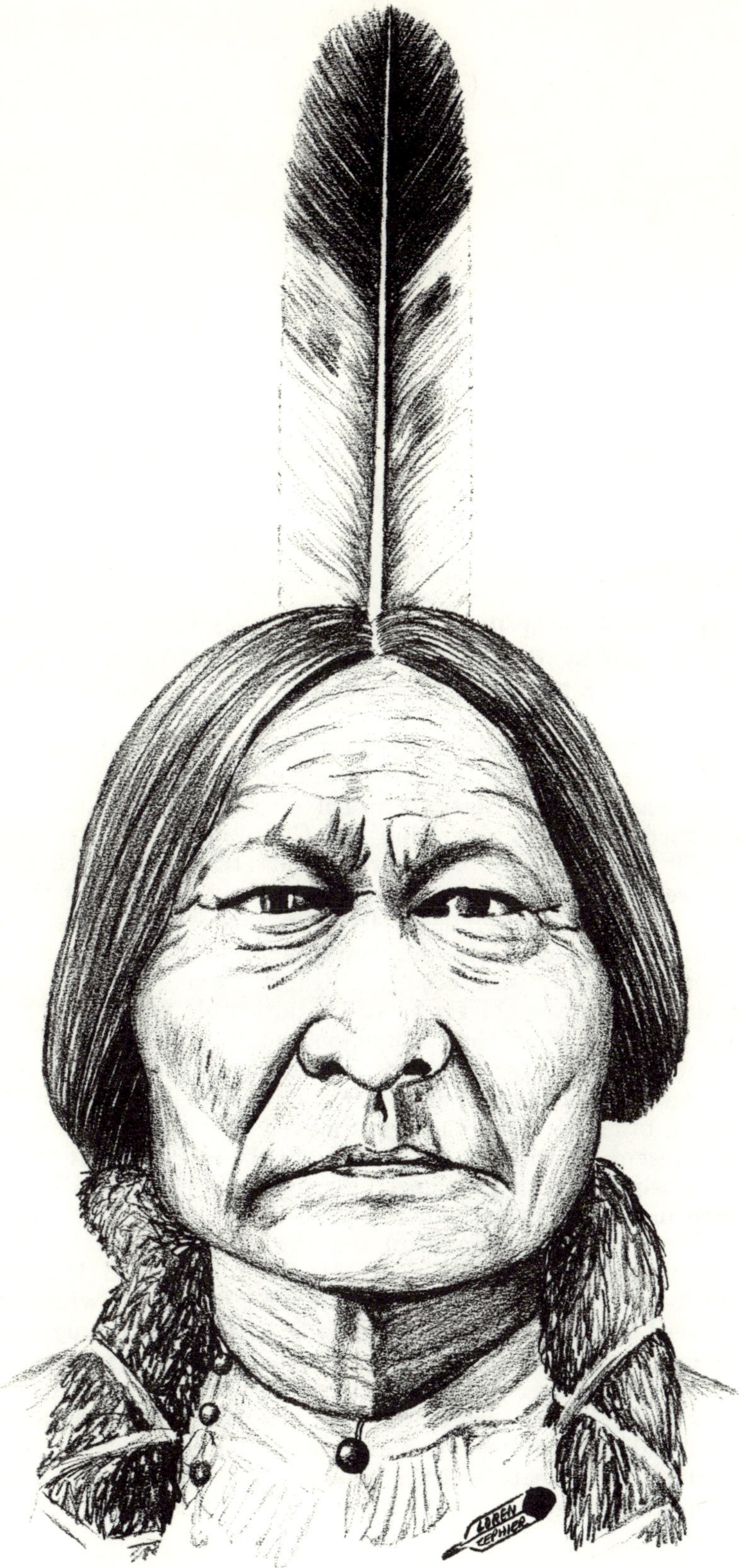

HUMP

1848-1908

Minneconjou Teton

Hump, the grandson of Black Buffalo who met Lewis and Clark in 1804, was considered by the United States agency officials to be even more dangerous than Sitting Bull in his hostility toward white ways and civilization.

After the Battle of the Little Big Horn, Hump assisted Crazy Horse in the Oglala's harrassment of General Crook until he and his band fled to Canada. He was one of the last to return to the United States.

Hump settled at Cherry Creek on the Cheyenne River Reservation with about 550 followers who stubbornly and strictly adhered to the old ways of dress, refused to cut their hair, openly performed the forbidden dances and lived in their issue tents in clustered villages. Hump frequently defied agency officials who were fearful of angering him.

Hump's people avidly embraced the Ghost Dance, but the Indian Police were so afraid of the chief who still retained his traditional leadership over his warriors, that they would not go to arrest him.

In November, 1890, after the military was again put in the control of the Sioux Reservation because of the fear that the Ghost Dance Movement would lead to an uprising, the army moved first against Hump considering him most dangerous of the old chiefs. However, the general in charge acted wisely preventing violence by sending Captain Ezra P. Ewers on the mission to Hump. Ewers, whom Hump trusted and liked, was sent all the way from Texas, so important did the military consider Hump. Ewers and only one other officer rode into Hump's camp. Hump was impressed by Ewer's courage in coming alone when the other whites were afraid and agreed to move his whole band to the agency. Although Hump and his warriors had many times defied the officials and practiced the Ghost Dance, they had never committed any violent act against the whites. At the agency Hump and several of his warriors were recruited as scouts to reach other Indians who practiced the new religion.

After Sitting Bull's death and the massacre at Wounded Knee, Hump became less hostile, accepted the white manner of dress, but never accepted Christianity.

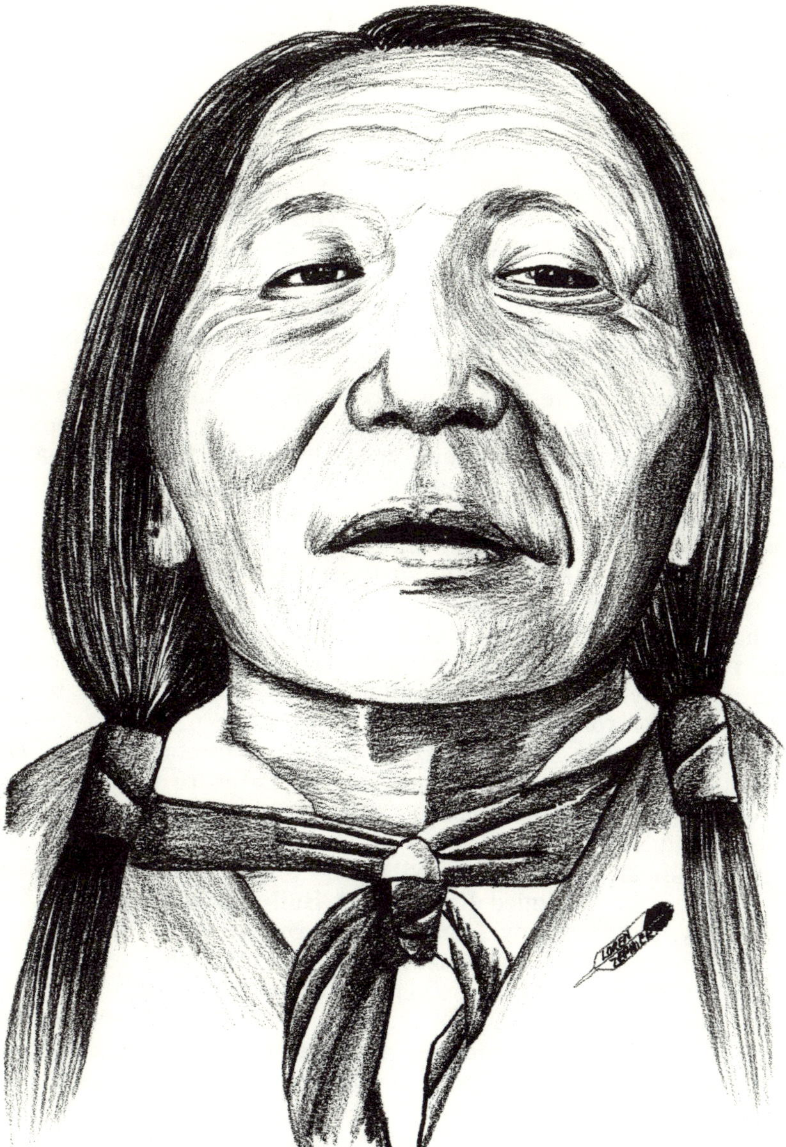

SHORT BULL

1840(?)-1900(?)

Brule Teton

Short Bull was a minor medicine man of Chief Lip's band. He was with Crazy Horse in 1876, but returned to the Rosebud to live on Pass Creek. When word reached the Teton of the new religion preached by Wovoka, Short Bull was one of the emissaries sent to the "Messiah" to learn of the Paiute's teachings. On his return to the Rosebud, Short Bull preached the Messiah's coming and taught the Brule the sacred songs and ritual of the Ghost Dance.

The first dance was held at Iron Creek on the Little White River. The participants danced until they fell into a swoon and while unconscious believed that they conversed with long dead chiefs, friends, and relatives. So intense was Short Bull's involvement in the tenets and ritual of the new religion that he came to believe that he was the "Messiah".

On October 31, 1890, a large encampment of dancers were gathered at Black Pipe Creek on the Rosebud and there Short Bull was seized with a fervent eloquence and proclaimed himself the Messiah. Wovoka had predicted that a great dust storm would come to destroy all of the whites and the land would once more be the Indians'. Short Bull advanced the time of the great storm to a date about December 11, 1890. He told the dancers that in order for the catastrophic event to occur they must keep faith, dance and wear the sacred shirts which were immune to the white men's bullets. In November Short Bull led the Brule to the Pine Ridge border to join with other Ghost Dancers and prepare for the dust storm.

The storm did not come and some of Short Bull's followers, wearing the protective "Ghost Shirts", fled with Big Foot into the Bad Lands. After the massacre at Wounded Knee Short Bull saw his followers lying dead in the snow, shirts bloody from the piercing of many bullets.

Short Bull surrendered to General Miles on January 16, 1891 and was sent to Fort Sheridan, Illinois where he was confined until the white men's panic over the Ghost Dance subsided. Short Bull was a sadly disillusioned man, but still considered a threat by the government. He was removed from his tribe and sent to Europe with Buffalo Bill's Wild West Show.

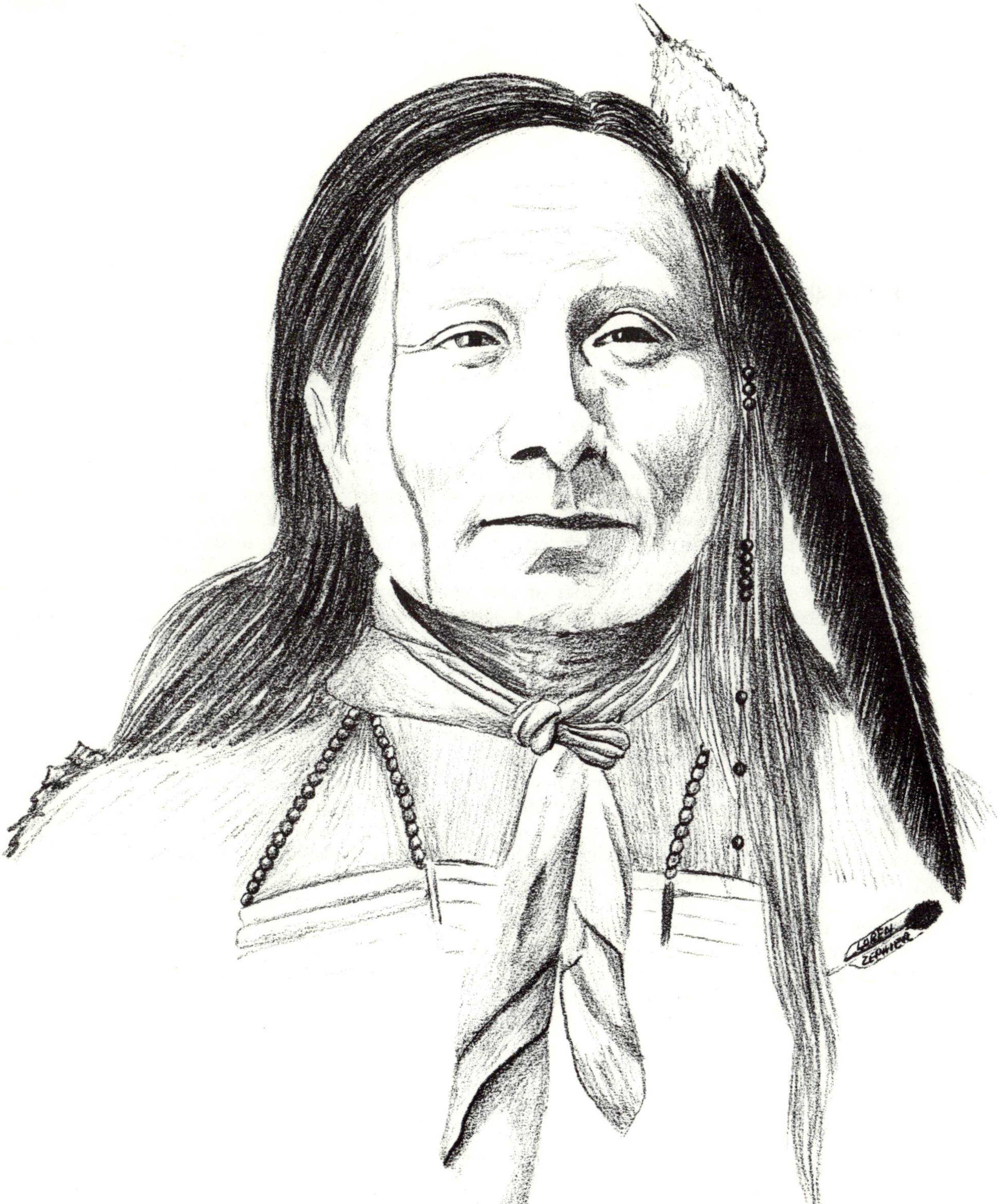
LOREN
ZEPHIER

GABRIEL RENVILLE

1825-1892

Sisseton Santee

Gabriel Renville was a mixed-blood Santee—his father was half French and his mother half Scot. Renville was the treaty chief of the Sisseton-Wahpeton Santee tribes and signed the 1867 treaty which established the boundaries of the Lake Traverse Reservation.

During the 1862 Uprising Renville opposed Little Crow and was influential in keeping many of the Santee out of the war. He served General Sibley as chief of scouts during the campaign against the Sioux in 1863.

Even though Renville was an ally of the whites, after he settled on the reservation he was considered hostile by the government agent, Moses N. Adams. Renville was the leader of the "scout party" which was in conflict with the "good church" Indians. Renville preserved many of the traditional Santee customs of polygamy and dancing, and he ignored Christianity. However, Renville was not opposed to economic progress and he and his followers became successful farmers on the reservation.

The Sisseton agent favored the "church" Indians and Renville and other leaders of the traditional Indians accused the agent of discriminating against them in the disposition of supplies and equipment. Renville said Adams favored the idle church-goers instead of encouraging them to work. Agent Adams considered Renville a detriment and removed the chief from the reservation executive board which the agent had organized to carry out his policies. This action was considered unnecessarily violent. In 1874 Renville was finally successful in securing a government investigation of the agent's activities which resulted in an official censure of Adams.

Renville continued to practice the old Santee customs, yet he encouraged the Indians to farm. This progressive influence was greatly missed after his death in August, 1892.

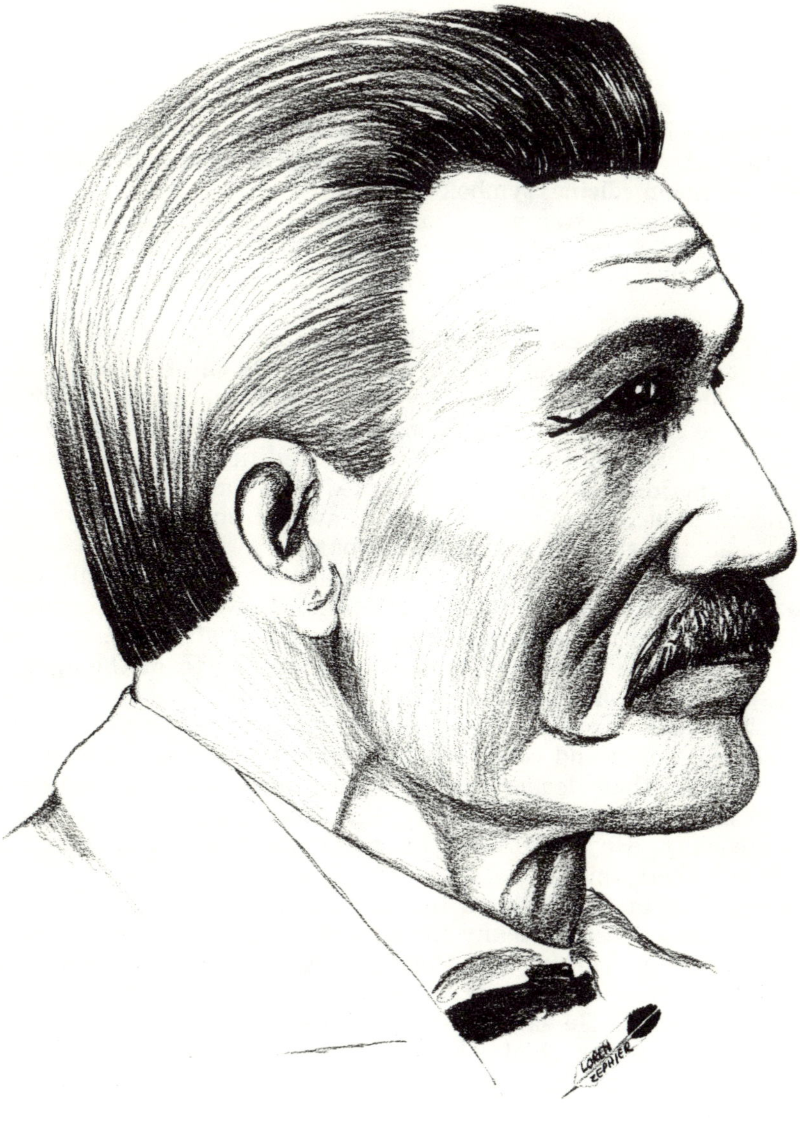
LOREN ZEPHIER

SINTE GALESKA, SPOTTED TAIL

1823(?)-1881

Brule Teton

This Brule chief's name was Jumping Buffalo, but he became known as Spotted Tail after a white trapper gave him a raccoon tail which he always wore as his medicine symbol.

Spotted Tail, whose sister was Crazy Horse's mother, was a skilled diplomat and his wiley dealings with officials finally located the Brule reservation at the Rosebud in the area Spotted Tail loved and considered home.

In 1879, Spotted Tail sent four of his sons and some of his grandchildren to the Carlisle Indian School in Pennsylvania. But after the children were baptized Episcopalian and given Christian names without his permission, he angrily removed them. He was not against education for the young, but wanted them to follow the traditional Brule customs and religion. A majority of the Sioux backed him and would not give up their children to be sent hundreds of miles away from home to become "white men" and forget their ethnic background.

The government built Spotted Tail a mansion which he and his four wives and many children lived in for some time. However, no furniture was included in the house and camping in the enclosed structure was not to the chief's liking. He moved his family to a camp north of the agency where he installed each of his wives in her own teepee.

Spotted Tail liked women, especially pretty young women. To the Brules, his several wives and conquests of young unmarried and married girls indicated that their leader was a strong man and they enjoyed gossiping and laughing about it. Spotted Tail loved all of his wives and treated them equally. He was fond of his numerous children and they in turn worshipped their father.

Crow Dog, chief of the Rosebud Indian Police, coveted Spotted Tail's power and tried unsuccessfully many times to subvert the old chief's leadership and influence in Washington. Finally in August of 1881, Crow Dog lost his position as chief of police because of Spotted Tail's influence and his envy became hatred. He saw Spotted Tail returning from the agency and treacherously shot the chief who fell from his horse. Spotted Tail staggered to his feet, drew his revolver and attempted to fire, but before he could, he fell dead at his rival's feet.

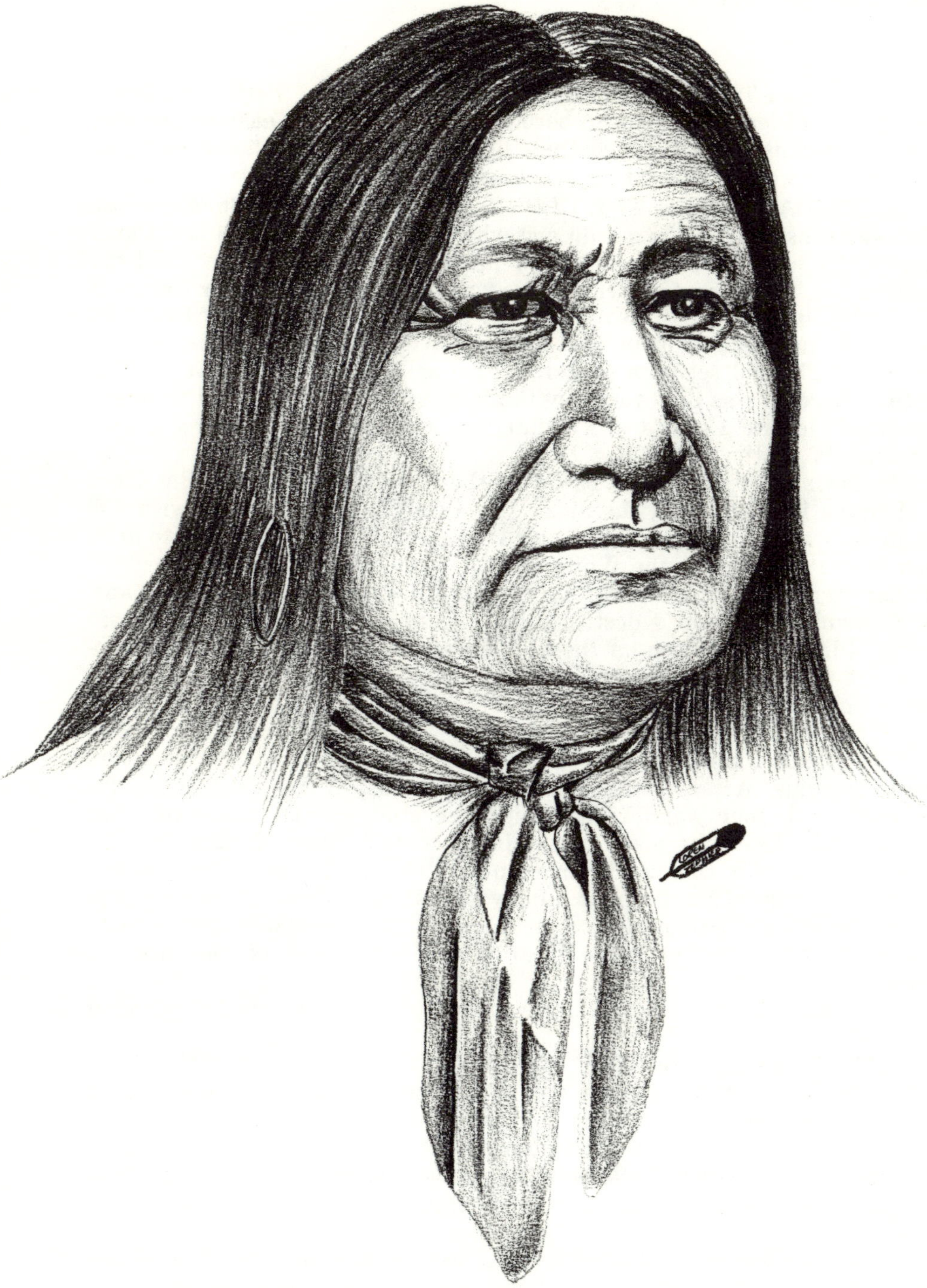

AMERICAN HORSE

The Elder, (?)-1876

The Younger, 1860(?)-(?)

Oglala Teton

Two Oglala Teton bore the name American Horse. Both were brave courageous leaders and given to heroic deeds. Thus, it is easy to see why many historians have recorded their lives as being that of one man; although they were a generation apart and not at all related.

AMERICAN HORSE, THE ELDER, was the son of Old Smoke whose band was considered to be a wild one which never went to the Red Cloud Agency. He was, however, a friend of Spotted Tail's and often visited the Brule leader. The elder American Horse was present at the Custer Battle at the Little Big Horn. Afterwards, he led his band towards Bear Butte intending to move on to winter at the Spotted Tail Agency. He had no desire to fight and set up a peaceful camp at Slim Buttes before moving south. There he was discovered by Captain Anson Mills and 150 troopers, a part of General Crook's army that was revengefully pursuing Indian participants of the Little Big Horn.

Following the disastrous battle of the Rosebud and Little Big Horn in Montana in June, 1876, the Sioux (save Gall and Sitting Bull with 400 lodges who went to Canada and Crazy Horse and his band) started to drift back to the agencies on the White and Missouri Rivers burning the grass as they went. Generals Crook, Terry and Miles started to hunt Indians. By September 7, Crook's destitute and weary column detached Captain Anson Mills with 150 men on the best horses to go to Deadwood for supplies. On the 8th he discovered a village on the east slope of Slim Buttes and at dawn on the 9th attacked the teepees, tightly buttoned up against the rain, with a cavalry charge, scattering the Indians.

The Oglala Chief, American Horse with 15 women and four warriors fled to a ravine. After a six hour siege where most of the white casualties occurred, with four warriors dead and the chief fatally wounded, they surrendered. That afternoon Crazy Horse made a show of force but the balance of Crook's command came up and there was no battle, only a constant harrassment. A great supply of valuable dried meat was captured, the village destroyed, and on the 10th the command moved on to Deadwood, on a diet of horse meat marking the end of the summer campaign.

American Horse, being fatally wounded in the groin, died September 14, 1876.

AMERICAN HORSE, THE YOUNGER, was the son of Sitting Bear and at his father's death became chief of the Oglala True Band. Crook tricked American Horse into signing the 1889 Treaty which none of the older chiefs would do and Red Cloud accused American Horse of betrayal. The younger American Horse was an eloquent orator who loved to talk. His endless harangues at meetings with white men drove them wild with impatience.

American Horse was considered a progressive by the Pine Ridge Agent, Major V. T. McGillycuddy, who appointed him head chief of the Oglalas in an attempt to break Red Cloud's power. The appointment was meaningless for the Oglalas still considered Red Cloud their leader and the younger man was ignored.

This portrait is of American Horse, the Younger.

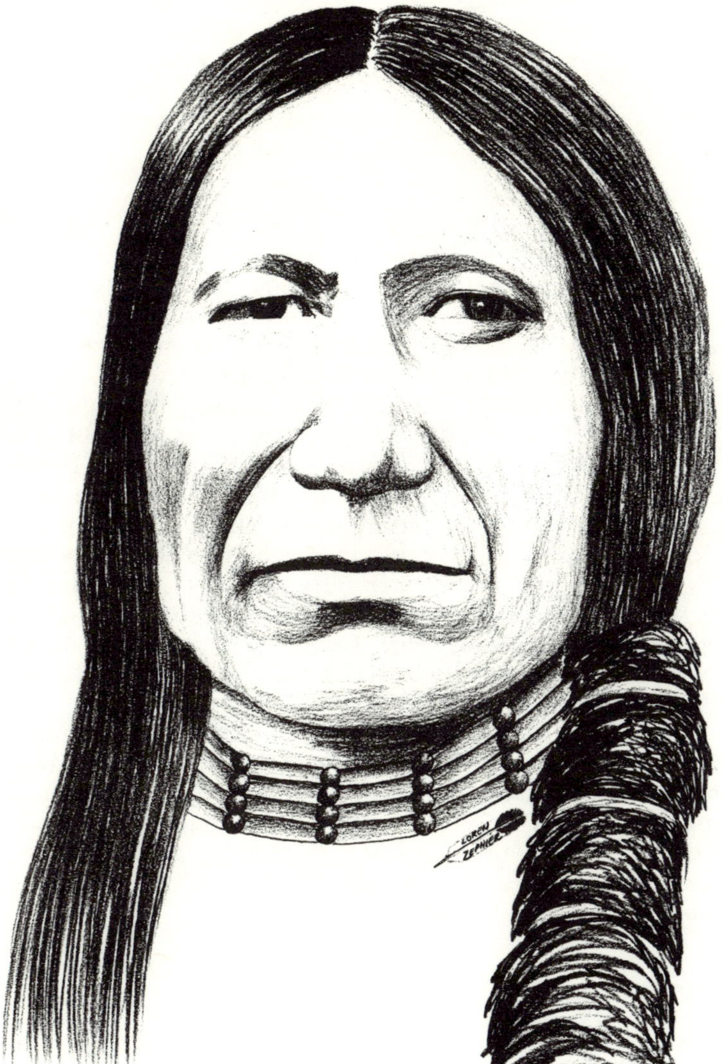
LOREN
ZEPHIER

MAHPIYATO, BLUE CLOUD

1833-1918

Yankton

Blue Cloud was the son of Flying Feather, daughter of Chief Hashata, and Major Jonathan Bean, the white sutler of the Ponca and Yankton Indians. Major Bean named the boy William, but soon deserted his Yankton wife and half-breed son. The boy was also unwanted by Flying Feather who left him to be raised by his grandfather while she joined the Hunkpapa Teton and was refuted to be one of Sitting Bull's wives.

Hashata named the boy Blue Cloud and raised him as a Yankton warrior. The old man was greatly influenced by the visit of explorer Jean Nicolet and later by the young Belgian priest, Pierre Jean DeSmet, so that both Hashata and his grandson were baptized Roman Catholic.

Blue Cloud worked as a scout and guide for the U. S. Army mapping expeditions on the Powder River and in Utah. During that time he searched unsuccessfully for his father. He traveled to Minatree and Mandan country with Father De Smet and also accompanied the priest to the 1851 treaty conference at Fort Laramie. During the Minnesota Uprising he was one of the scouts sent by Struck By The Ree to warn white settlers and worked to keep the Yankton peaceful.

In 1877 he was appointed head chief by the government agents after the hereditary leader, Felix Brunot, son of Pretty Boy, left the tribe.

Blue Cloud was a man of peace and a devout Roman Catholic who remained a staunch supporter of his faith even though his people were without a priest for fifty years. He saw Christianity as a way for peace with the white men and worked all of his life for that end and for what he believed was the good of his people.

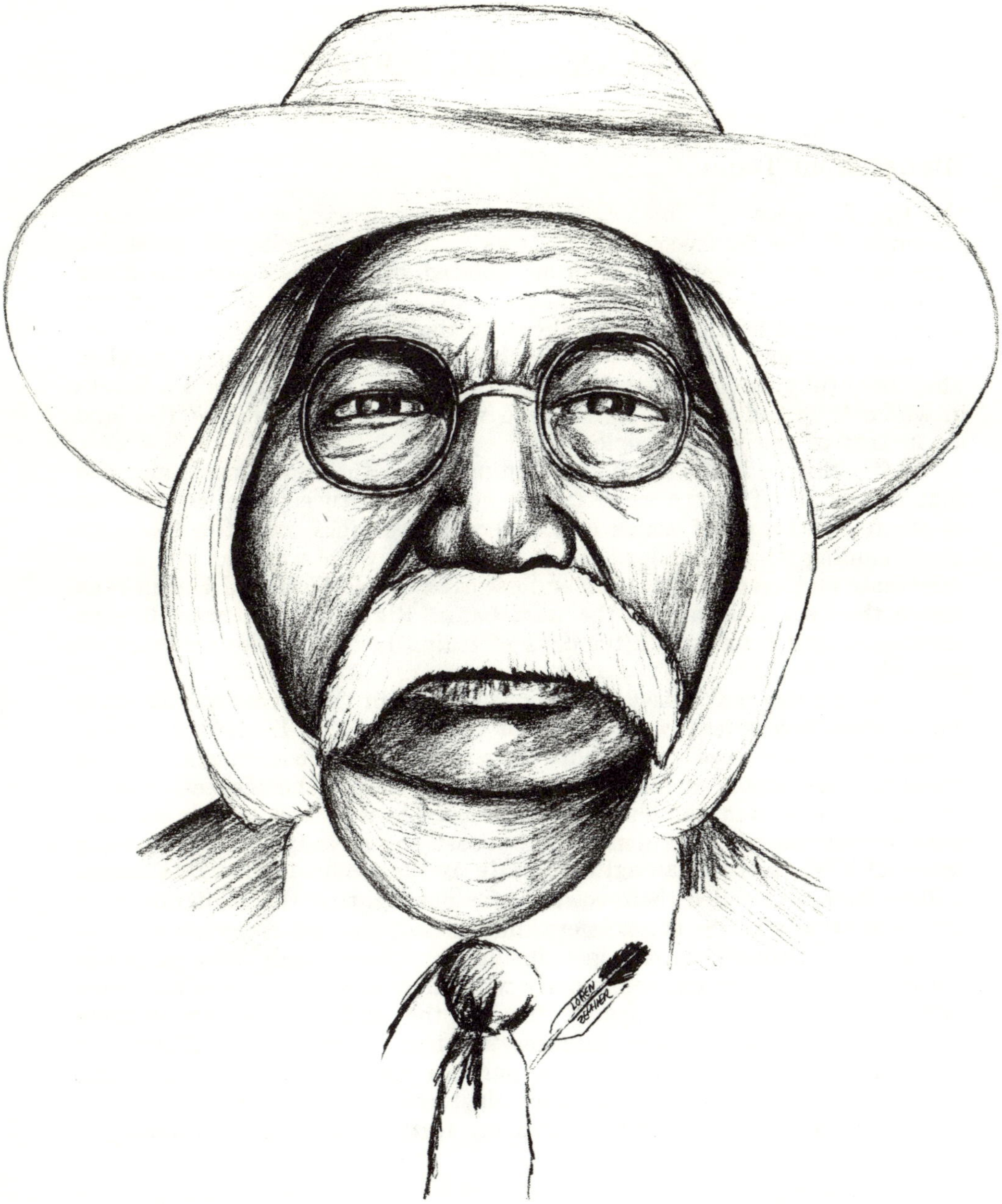
LOREN

SITANKA, BIG FOOT

18(?)-1890

Minneconjou Teton

Big Foot, son of Chief Lone Horn of the North, was a hereditary headman of the Minneconjou. He was active in the Sioux's defensive wars of 1876 and later settled in an isolated site on the Cheyenne River Reservation. He and his band remained holdouts against civilization and were considered hostile troublemakers by the government.

Big Foot and his people readily accepted the Ghost Dance religion. They faithfully performed the hypnotic dance and many fell into a trance in which they had visions of the dead who came to life and of the land again free of the white people.

After Sitting Bull's death at Standing Rock, Big Foot became alarmed that he would suffer the same fate if he were captured. He led a group of about 340 Teton, of which only 106 were warriors, into the Badlands after eluding U. S. Troops. They were finally intercepted by Major Whiteside on December 28, 1890 and escorted to the Wounded Knee Creek where they set up camp on the west bank. Big Foot, who was ill with pneumonia and exhausted after days of riding in bitter cold, surrendered willingly.

A white flag was raised as a sign of peace in the center of the camp which was surrounded by soldiers. On the morning of December 29, the warriors were ordered to give up their weapons. When only a few old muskets were produced the soldiers began to search the teepees, greatly alarming the women and children who began to wail and scream as they were turned out of their homes. This upset the already uneasy warriors who had been roused to an agitated state by the medicine man Zitkalazizi, Yellow Bird, who called them cowards for not fighting the soldiers.

A shot was fired. The soldiers immediately opened fire directly into the warriors gathered in one spot during the search. Half were instantly killed. The others fought desperately with their hands, but were also soon killed. A Hotchkiss gun opened fire on the gathering of the women and children. In only a few minutes 200 men, women and children lay dead. The survivors fled, but were pursued and shot down. Big Foot's body and those of the warriors were clustered in the camp's center, but the bodies of the women and children lay scattered for miles around.

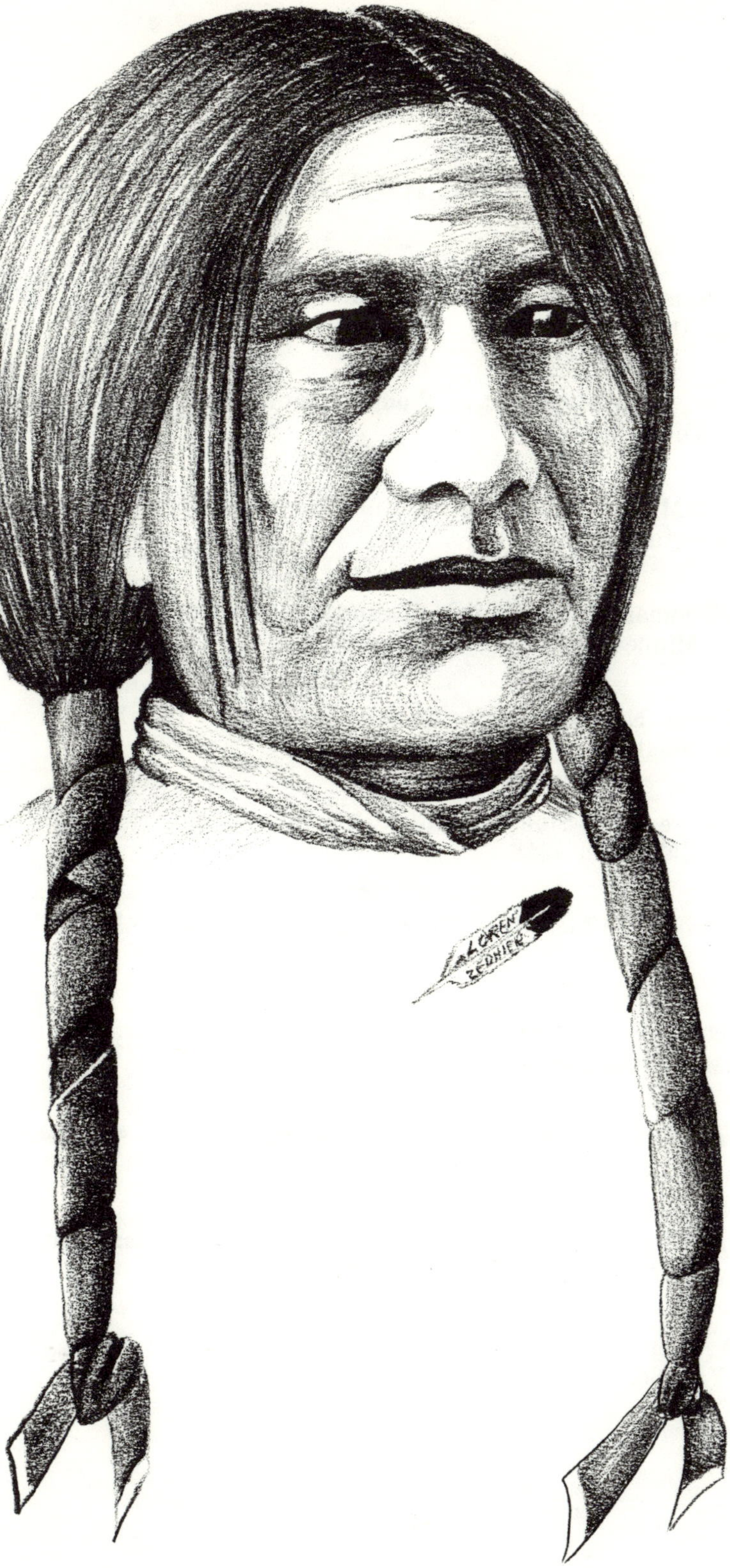
LOREN
ZEPHIER

BIBLIOGRAPHY

Brevet's South Dakota Historical Markers, Brevet Press, Sioux Falls, South Dakota 1974.

Brown, Dee, **Bury My Heart at Wounded Knee,** Holt, Rinehart & Winston, New York, N. Y. 1970.

Hans, Fred M., **The Great Sioux Nation,** Ross, Haines reprint, Minneapolis, Minnesota 1964.

Hughes, Thomas, **Indian Chiefs of Southern Minnesota,** Free Press, Mankato, Minnesota 1927.

Hyge, George E., **Red Cloud's Folk,** University of Oklahoma Press, Norman, Oklahoma 1967.

Hyde, George E., **A Sioux Chronicle,** University of Oklahoma Press, Norman, Oklahoma 1956.

Larkin, Georgia, **Chief Blue Cloud,** Blue Cloud Abby, Marvin, South Dakota 1964.

Meyer, Roy W., **History of the Santee Sioux,** University of Nebraska Press, Lincoln, Nebraska 1967.

Robinson, Doane, **Encyclopedia of South Dakota,** Will A. Beach Printing Co., Sioux Falls, South Dakota 1925.

Robinson, Doane, **A History of the Dakota or Sioux Indians,** Ross & Haines reprint, Minneapolis, Minnesota 1967.

Roland, Albert, **Great Indian Chiefs,** Crowell-Collier Press, New York, N. Y. 1966.

A
Adams, Moses N. — 34
Alleghenies — 2
American Horse — 38
American Horse, the Younger — 38
American Revolutionary War — 2, 4, 12
Apadani — 10
Arikara — 2
Ash Hollow Massacre — 3, 14

B
Bad Faces Band — 24
Badlands — 32, 42
Bad River — 18
Bean, Major Jonathan — 38
Bear Butte — 38
Belle Fourche River — 3
Benteen, Captain Frederick W. — 20
Big Foot — 28, 32, 42
Big Mound — 16, 20
Big Sioux River — 3
Big Stone Lake — 21
Bismarck — 20
Black Buffalo — 30
Black Buffalo Woman — 26
Black Hills — 3, 22, 26
Black Hills War — 3
Blackfeet — 2
Black Pipe Creek — 32
Blue Cloud — 40
Bozeman Trail — 3
British — 2, 4, 6, 8
Brule — 2, 3, 14, 26, 36, 38
Brunot, Felix — 40
Buford, Fort — 20
Bull Head, Lieutenant — 28
Butcher, The — 14
Butte County — 3

C
Calument Bluff — 10
Canada — 12, 20, 38
Carlisle Indian School — 36
Catch the Bear — 28
Catholic, Roman — 24, 40
Charger, Martin — 18
Charles-Mix County — 10
Cherry Creek — 30
Cheyenne, Northern — 26, 27
Cheyenne River — 3
Cheyenne River Reservation — 28, 30, 42
Chippewa-Sioux Boundary Conference — 4
Chippawas — 1, 2, 4, 6
Choteau Creek — 10
Christianity — 40
Clark, Governor — 8
Crawford, Winona — 4
Clark, William — 10, 18, 30
Cody, Buffalo Bill — 28, 32
Conquering Bear — 26
Corn Band — 14
Crazy Horse — 20, 26, 27, 32, 36, 38
Crazy Horse's people — 27
Crook, General George — 3, 27, 30, 38
Crow Creek — 3
Crow Dog — 26
Crow Foot — 28
Custer, General G. A. — 3, 20, 27, 28

D
Dakota — 1, 3, 4
Deadwood — 38
DeSmet, Pierre Jean — 40
Duley, Mrs. Laura (William) — 18

E
Eatoka — 6
Elm River Battle — 6
Episcopalian — 12, 18, 36
Everett, Lillian — 18
Ewers, Captain Ezra P. — 30

F
Fetterman, Colonel — 26
First Minnesota Mounted Rangers — 20
Flandreau, So. Dak. — 12
Flying Feather — 40
Fool Soldiers — 18
Forsyth, Major George A. — 6
French — 1, 6, 8

G
Galbraith — 12
Gall — 20, 38
Gardner, Abbie — 16
Ghost Dance — 3, 20, 22, 24, 30, 42
Ghost Shirts — 32
Grand River — 2, 18
Grattan Battle of 1854 — 26
Grattan, Lieutenant J. L. — 26
Great Lakes — 2
Great Spirit — 26
Gulf of Mexico — 2

H
Half Dozen, The — 6
Harding County — 3
Harney, William S. 3, 14
Hashata — 40
Hochokaduta — 6
Hotchkiss — 42
Hudson's Bay — 2
Hump — 30
Hunkpapa — 2, 20
Hunkpapa Teton — 40
Hunkpatila — 22
Huron — 1
Hutchinson — 12

I
Illinois — 2, 32
Ilges, Major Guido — 20, 32
Inkpaduta — 16, 20
Iowa — 4
Iowas — 2, 3, 16
Ireland, Ella — 18
Ireland, Rosanna — 18
Iron Creek — 32
Isanti — 1
Itazipo — 2

J
James River — 2, 8
Jumping Buffalo — 36

K
Kills Game and Comes Back — 18

L
Lake Pipin — 4
Lake Shetek Massacre — 18
Lake Superior — 6
Lake Traverse Reservation — 34
Lakota — 1, 2
Laramie, Fort — 3, 24, 40
Laramie Treaty — 3
Le Demi Douzen — 6
Lewis, Meriwether — 10, 18, 30
Lip — 32
Lisa, Manuel — 8
Little Big Horn — 3, 16, 20, 27, 28, 30, 38
Little Crow — 6, 12, 34
Little Powder River — 26
Little Thunder — 14
Little White River — 32
Loafer Band — 14
Lone Horn — 42
Lott, Henry — 16
Lower Agency — 12

Mc
McGillycuddy, Major V. T. — 22, 24, 38
McLaughlin, James — 20

M
Mackinaw, Michigan — 4
Mahpialuta — 24
Man Afraid of His Horses — 22
Mandan — 40
Marble, Margaret Ann — 16
Mdeisanti — 1
Mdewakanton — 1
Meade County — 3
Medicine Man — 28
Mendota, Treaty of — 3
Messiah — 32
Miles, General Nelson A. — 20, 22, 27, 32, 38
Mille Lacs — 1
Mills, Captain Anson — 38
Minatree — 40
Minneconjou — 2, 42
Minnesota — 1, 2, 3, 4, 6, 16
Minnesota Massacre — 4
Minnesota Reservation — 12
Minnesota State Historical Society — 12

45

Minnesota Uprising of 1862 — 3, 4, 12, 16, 18, 34, 42
Minnesota Valley — 2, 3
Mississippi River — 1, 2, 4, 8
Missouri — 4
Missouri Ponca Agency — 14
Missouri River — 2, 3, 8, 10, 27, 38
Mongolian — 1
Montana — 38
Moreau River — 20
Mormon's cow — 26

N

Nadewisou — 1
Nakota — 2
Nebraska Reservation — 4
Nicolet, Jean — 1, 40
North Dakota — 2
Northern Pacific Railroad — 3

O

Oak Creek — 20
Objibwa — 1, 6
Oglala — 2, 3, 14, 22, 24, 26, 37, 38
Oglala Teton — 38
Oglala True Band — 38
Okoboji — 16
Old Man Afaid of His Horses — 22
Old Smoke — 38
Old Strike — 10
Omahas — 2
One-Eyed Sioux, The — 8
Oohenumpa — 2
Otonwahe — 1
Ottawa — 2
Overland Trail — 14

P

Pacific Coast — 10
Padaniapapi — 10
Paiute — 32
Palaneape — 10
Pass Creek — 32
Payaba — 22
Pennsylvania — 36
Perkins County — 3
Pierre, Fort — 18
Pike, Lieutenant Zebulon Montgomery — 4, 8
Pike's Treaty — 2
Pine Ridge — 22, 24, 38
Pizi — 20
Platte River — 14
Ponca Indians — 40
Pond, S. W. Jr. — 6
Pontiac — 2
Pontiac War — 2, 4
Popular River — 20
Portages des Sioux — 4
Powder River — 24, 27, 40
Prairie du Chien — 2, 4, 8
Pretty Boy — 40
Pushed Aside — 22

R

Radisson, Pierre — 1
Randall, Fort — 28
Rapid Creek — 26
Red Cloud — 3, 22, 24, 26, 27, 38
Red Cloud Agency — 38
Red Cloud War — 3, 20
Red Tomahawk — 28
Red Wing — 4
Red Wood River — 6
Ree — 2
Reno, Major Marcus A. — 20
Renville, Gabriel — 4, 34
Reynolds, Colonel J. J. — 26, 27
Rising Elk — 8
Rising Moose — 8
Robinson, Fort — 27
Rocky Mountains — 2
Rosebud — 30, 36, 38
Rosebud, Battle of the — 3, 27
Rosebud Indian police — 36

S

St. Croix River — 2
St. Louis — 8
St. Paul — 4
Santee — 1, 2, 3, 4, 6, 8, 10, 12, 16, 18, 34
Sans Arc — 2
Shakopee — 6
Sheridan, Fort — 32
Shooter, the — 4

Short Bull — 32
Sibley, General Henry Hastings — 18, 20, 34
Sicangu — 2
Sihasapa — 2
Sioux — 1, 4
Sioux Nation — 1
Sioux Reservation — 3, 20, 24
Sioux River — 2
Sisseton — 1, 2, 3, 20
Sisseton Treaty — 3
Sisseton-Wahpeton Santee — 34
Sitting Bear — 38
Sitting Bull — 20, 27, 28, 30, 38, 40, 42
Slim Buttes — 3, 38
Snelling, Fort — 6
South American — 1
South Dakota — 3
Spirit Lake Massacre — 16
Spotted Tail — 26, 36, 38
Spotted Tail Agency — 14, 27, 38
Standing Rock — 42
Standing Rock Reservation — 20, 28
Struck By The Ree — 10, 40
Sun Dance — 29

T

Tamaha — 8
Taoya Te Duta — 12
Tasagi — 16
Tashunka Witco — 26
Tashunkopipape — 22
Tatankamani — 4
Terry, General Alfred — 38
Teton — 1, 2, 3, 18, 20, 22, 32, 42
Traverse des Sioux, Treaty of — 2, 3, 4
Treaty of 1805 — 8
Treaty of 1837 — 4
Treaty of 1851 — 6
Treaty of 1858 — 10
Treaty of 1889 — 3, 20, 22, 24, 38
Treaty Conference of 1851 — 40
Turkey Head — 18
Two Kettle — 2, 18
Two Moon — 20

U

Uncpapa — 2
United States Army — 3, 40

W

Wabasha — 4
Wabasha, Minnesota — 8
Wacouta — 4
Wahpekute — 1, 16
Wahpeton — 1, 3
Wakantanka — 26, 28
Wakpala — 20
Walking Buffalo — 4
Wamdesapa — 16
War of 1812 — 6, 8
Washington, D. C. — 24
Weiser, Dr. Joseph S. — 16, 20
White Beard — 14
White Lodge — 18
White River — 3, 38
White Stone Hill — 16
Whiteside, Major Federick — 42
Wiciyela — 2
Wild West Show — 28, 32
Winnebago — 1
Wisconsin — 2, 4
Woinapa — 12
Wolf Mountains — 27
Wood Lake Battle — 6, 12
Wounded Knee — 22, 24, 30, 32
Wounded Knee Creek — 42
Wounded Knee Massacre — 3, 42
Wovoka — 32
Wowacinye — 18
Wright, Dora — 18
Wright, Mrs. Julia (John) — 18
Wyoming — 4

Y

Yankton — 1, 2, 3, 10, 40
Yankton Treaty — 3
Yellow Bird — 42
Yellowstone — 28
Young Man Afraid of His Horses — 22

Z

Zitkalazizi — 42